THE TITANIC DISASTER

THE TITANIC DISASTER

OMENS, MYSTERIES AND MISFORTUNES OF THE DOOMED LINER

JAMES W BANCROFT

FRONTLINE
BOOKS

First published in Great Britain in 2023 by
FRONTLINE BOOKS
an imprint of Pen & Sword Books Ltd,
47 Church Street, Barnsley, S. Yorkshire, S70 2AS

ISBN: 978-1-39904-895-8

For more information on our books, please visit
www.frontline-books.com, email info@frontline-books.com
or write to us at the above address.

Printed and bound by CPI Group (UK) Ltd, Croydon, CR0 4YY
Typeset by Concept, Huddersfield, West Yorkshire
Pen & Sword Books Ltd incorporates the imprints of Pen & Sword
Archaeology, Atlas, Aviation, Battleground, Discovery,
Family History, History, Maritime, Military, Naval, Politics,
Social History, Transport, True Crime, Claymore Press,
Frontline Books, Praetorian Press,
Seaforth Publishing and White Owl

For a complete list of Pen and Sword titles please contact
PEN & SWORD LTD
47 Church Street, Barnsley, South Yorkshire, S70 2AS, England
E-mail: enquiries@pen-and-sword.co.uk

Or

PEN AND SWORD BOOKS
1950 Lawrence Rd, Havertown, PA 19083, USA
E-mail: Uspen-and-sword@casematepublishers.com

CONTENTS

INTRODUCTION

An equally appropriate title for this book could have been *A Diary of Misfortune*. There are more strange events concerning RMS *Titanic* than any other ship in history, and the feelings of foreboding and bad omens associated with it suggest that fate had it doomed to a watery grave; the iceberg just being the weapon that sent it there. The story of RMS *Titanic* is shrouded in mystery and steeped in intrigue.

For instance, a novel written many years before *Titanic* was built mirrored almost exactly the details of the disaster, and many people left accounts expressing their concerns about the vessel. Even a dog seems to have sensed danger and tried to stop its owner from travelling to the ship. It may also be stated that so many unusual things are said to have occurred that there must be an element of truth in some of them. Certainly many of the stories are thought-provoking; and the disaster still maintains a powerful grip on the public's imagination.

If something associated with *Titanic* caused misfortune, was it connected with the Harland and Wolff shipyard; the White Star Line; the captain or another person, or a cursed item stored on board? Could they all be urban legends? Why were there so many omens of foreboding? Did several people who lost their lives in the disaster return from the other side to tell their experiences? I have addressed some of these points with my own thoughts and theories. For instance, could it have been Captain Edward Smith who was seen alive soon after the disaster? And was there indeed a cursed Egyptian artefact on the ship?

However, this is not an analysis or exposé. I do not have a PhD in psychical research, nor am I a member of any society that studies things like unexplained phenomena; not that they would make any difference. Like most people who have an interest in *Titanic* matters, my credentials are the fact that I have read and listened to everything I possibly could about the dreadful disaster, especially concerning the people who were involved, in my case for over four decades, and many of these events came to my notice while I was writing *Titanic: Iceberg Ahead – The Story of the Disaster by Some of Those Who Were There*.

In addition to official documentation and first-hand statements, I have used newspaper reports, and although they contain inaccuracies that modern research has brought to light, they have been a valuable source, bringing much into perspective, and they have formed the basis for the general information concerning the tragedy used by researchers over the years. In the days of limited technology a newspaper was the main source of information for the public, and it is interesting to learn how people got to know about the events and how the stories developed in the months after the tragedy. Many of the reports appear here for the first time since they were originally published, and for more lucidity, I have related the stories in chronological order as much as possible.

Lawrence Beesley, a Derbyshire science teacher who survived the sinking, stated:

> One more thing must be referred to – the prevalence of superstitious beliefs concerning the Titanic. I suppose no ship ever left port with so much miserable nonsense showered on her. In the first place, there is no doubt many people refused to sail on her because it was her maiden voyage, and this apparently is a common superstition; even the clerk of the White Star Office, where I purchased my ticket, admitted it was a reason that prevented people from sailing. A number of people have written to the press to say they had thought of sailing on her, but because of 'Omens' cancelled the passage. Many referred to the sister ship, the Olympic, pointed to the 'ill-luck' that they say has dogged her – her collision with the Hawke, and a second mishap necessitating repairs and a wait in harbour, where passengers deserted her.
>
> They prophesied even greater disaster for the Titanic, saying they would not dream of travelling on the boat. Even some aboard were very nervous in an undefined way. One lady said she had never wished to take this boat, but her friends had insisted and bought her ticket, and she had not had a happy moment since. A friend told me of the voyage of the Olympic from Southampton after the wait in harbour, and said there was a sense of gloom pervading the whole ship; the stewards and stewardesses even going as far as to say it was a 'death ship.' The crew, by the way, was largely transferred to the Titanic.

One person was lucky enough to miss the *Titanic* voyage after having a premonitory dream of disaster, something he had not experienced before, 'Crossing the Atlantic is nothing new to me, as I have crossed it a dozen times during the last few years, and I never remember having any feeling of uneasiness when about to do so or during the passage.' Another regular traveller on ships who was booked on *Titanic* seems to have sensed foreboding, stating that he had 'never had such a peculiar and constant feeling of impending trouble'.

Edward Smith took over as captain of *Titanic* on 1 April (the day of hoaxes), and as if throwing in the face of superstitious conformity, seven and thirteen, the two numbers synonymous with good and bad luck were turned on their heads during the incident, as the collision with the iceberg occurred during the ship's 'seven bells' watch, and thirteen lifeboats managed to carry the survivors to safety. Joseph Scarrott, a crewman who survived the disaster, stated, 'I signed the articles as 'A B' on Monday, 8 April 1912 – note the total of numbers in the year . . .'

I consider myself to be 90 per cent sceptic. Which is a strange statement to make of course – you either believe or you don't? But is it not that small element of possibility that keeps many of us intrigued by the subject? The other 10 per cent is based on one event I have never been able to comprehend. In my younger days I performed in a musical group that included two of my brothers, and we had a publicity photograph produced that included the five people who made up the group. When my brother died, my wife pencil-sketched a picture of him taking his image alone from the photograph. Some years later we became aware of a lady who apparently could make contact with people from the other side by holding an item associated with them. There was no financial gain involved. My wife took the sketch of my brother to her to see if she could make contact with him. There was no way she could have known about the original group photograph, but as soon as she touched the sketch she remarked, 'There should be some other people in this picture.' She did make contact with him in her mind's eye, and everything she said about how he was behaving reflected his character.

I have tried to present the incidents with an open mind, with the aim of being informative as opposed to controversial, although I have given my views on some of the stories and what might have influenced them. I leave it for the reader to consider why that one vessel more than any other had such a cloud of impending doom looming over it that seemed to make its dreadful fate inevitable.

James W Bancroft, 2023

1. TITANIC DISASTER

RMS *Titanic* was a Liverpool-registered ocean liner built for the transatlantic passenger and Royal Mail service, between Southampton, Cherbourg, Queenstown and New York. She was constructed at the massive Harland and Wolff shipyard in Belfast (see Appendix I) and was launched on 31 May 1911. She was the second of three Olympic-class liners, the first being RMS *Olympic*, which was constructed next to *Titanic* in the dock and sailed on its maiden voyage on 14 June 1911. The third ship in the class was RMS *Britannic*, which was laid down on 30 November 1911, but it was not launched until 26 February 1914 and went into service as a Great War hospital ship on 23 December 1915.

Titanic was valued at £1.5 million. She included sixteen watertight compartments featuring doors that could be closed automatically from the bridge, sealing off the compartments if necessary; the ship would still stay afloat even if four of the compartments were to flood. This system prompted people of the White Star Line to describe the vessel as 'practically unsinkable'. She officially entered service on 2 April 1912.

She was meant to accommodate about 3,000 passengers and over 900 crew members, and being a Royal Mail ship, she was carrying almost as many sacks of mail as people. One of the liner's four funnels served no purpose other than the fact that the designers thought the ship would look more impressive with four funnels rather than just three.

The ship was designed to provide the ultimate in luxury travel. There was a swimming pool with an adjacent Turkish bath suite, a state-of-the-art gymnasium, an à la carte restaurant, and the Café Parisien. However, the ship's main feature was the Grand Staircase. Built from solid English oak, and enhanced with wrought iron, the decorated glass domes above were designed to let in as much natural light as possible. To have sailed on 'the voyage of the century' aboard RMS *Titanic*, the world's largest and most luxurious vessel afloat at that time, was like being one of the first people to fly on Concorde. It was described at the time as 'a floating palace'.

One of the first recorded omens came to light when it was said that *Titanic*'s hull number was 390904 and its mirror image on the surface of the water in the dock looked similar to the words 'nopope'. This was taken by some of the more superstitious workers at the shipyard as a bad omen, and the ship suffered bad luck even before it started on its main journey across the Atlantic Ocean. A fire broke out in the coal bunkers before *Titanic* had even left Belfast, which the below-deck workers were desperately trying to get under control. She arrived at Southampton on Tuesday, 3 April 1912. She almost collided with another large vessel, SS *New York*, as she was leaving the harbour at Southampton on Wednesday, 10 April 1912.

Under the heading 'Titanic's Maiden Voyage' – newspapers reported on her departure and the incident that almost put a stop to her first journey:

The giant liner Titanic of the White Star fleet sailed from Southampton on April 11 *(sic)*, on her maiden voyage to New York. She had 300 first-class, 330 second-class, and 700 third-class passengers – a large company for a westward voyage at this time of the year – besides a crew numbering nearly 800. With a displacement of 46,328 tons – over 1,000 tons more than her sister ship Olympic – Titanic is the largest vessel afloat. From bow to stern she measures 882 feet 9 inches, and to inspect her thoroughly from end to end a four and a half mile walk would be necessary. So easy it is to get lost within the ship, that plans of her galleries and cabins have been placed in each of her decks.

The ship is really like a seagoing holiday resort, so many are the opportunities for recreation and amusement on board. Band concerts are frequent from morning till night. For passengers who want a strenuous life there is a deep sea-water swimming bath, a rackets court with a professional in charge, and a gymnasium under a qualified instructor, who will give lessons in physical culture and boxing. The gymnasium is also equipped with appliances whereby the pleasures of cycling, horse and camel riding, and rowing may be enjoyed.

The pre-eminence of the Titanic is not to remain unchallenged. The new Hamburg-American liner Imperator, which is shortly to be launched, will have a gross tonnage of 50,000, a length overall of 900 feet, and will accommodate 5,000 persons, with a promenade deck a quarter of a mile long. She will have an entertainment hall two stories high, holding 700 guests, a winter garden, and a Ritz-Carlton restaurant. The Cunard liner Aquitania, now building at Clydebank, Glasgow, is also a vessel of 50,000 tons.

The departure of the huge White Star liner Titanic, the largest ship in the world, on her maiden voyage to New York, with nearly 1,400 passengers on board, was almost marred by a disaster similar to that which befell the Olympic last September. Leaving her dock soon after noon, the Titanic in every sense a floating palace, was pulled out into Southampton Water by three tugs. Very slowly she passed alongside the quay. First she passed the liner Oceanic – a distance of about fifty yards separating the vessels – then she came opposite the liner New York.

Then it was that the seven ropes holding the New York to the quay began to strain. That she was being drawn towards the passing liner by suction could not be doubted. Suddenly there was a noise like minute guns going off. The seven ropes holding the New York to the quay had broken. Immediately the stern of the vessel began to veer round towards the Titanic. Then could be heard hasty megaphone orders aboard the liner, and many of the passengers appeared to be in a state of great excitement. Presently, the Titanic came to a standstill, and as soon as the rope had been disconnected the three tugs went to the assistance of the New York. At this time barely 15 feet separated the two vessels. Fortunately, the tugs were able to secure the New York and get her back to the quay.

Under her own steam *Titanic* backed about 200 yards. Eventually the three tugs were connected to the liner again, and another start was made, the liners being passed this time without mishap.

The ship travelled eastward and made her first port of call at Cherbourg in France, and then westward to Queenstown on the south coast of Ireland (now called Cobh). As she made her way out to sea from Queenstown, Fourth Officer Joseph Boxhall paused for thought as he noticed it was unusual that there were no sea birds flying around the ship as they usually did when they left a harbour.

Titanic continued on its voyage across the North Atlantic Ocean, and was making very good time. However, during the 'seven bells' watch, just before midnight on Sunday, 14 April 1912, she began to send out signals of distress, stating: 'We have struck an iceberg.' The ship had collided with an enormous body of ice that stripped off her bilge under the waterline for more than a hundred yards, opened up five of the front compartments and flooded the coal bunker servicing one of the boilers. The ship that took three years to build took less than three hours to sink.

According to sketches produced from the observations of teenage passenger Jack Thayer, the ship hit the iceberg at 12.45am, and the lifeboats were ordered to be launched about twenty minutes later. It broke in half at about 1.40am and the forward end sank soon afterwards. At two o'clock: 'Stern section pivots amidships and swings over spot where forward section sank.' The stern stayed upright for a short time and then plunged down into the water and was gone. No human eye would see it again for over seventy years.

3

There were sixteen lifeboats and four collapsible dinghies, which were insufficient, as a consequence of which two out of every three people on board perished. It was one of the deadliest peacetime maritime disasters in modern history. Over 300 bodies were picked up by ships in the following months after the disaster. Of those who went down with the ship, their bodies are now part of the ocean that consumed them.

The CS *Carpathia* was on its way from New York to Gibraltar and fortunately was in the region. On receiving a distress signal from *Titanic* it immediately set a heroic course towards the disaster area. After working through dangerous ice fields, it arrived at the scene at four o'clock in the morning of 15 April. Some people, mostly women and children, had escaped from *Titanic* in lifeboats and *Carpathia* saved over 700 of them.

The following report appeared in London newspapers concerning the sinking of *Titanic*, which was published on Tuesday, 16 April 1912 under the rather optimistic headline – 'Titanic Sunk. Many Persons Saved':

Reports received from the American side of the Atlantic state that the mammoth White Star liner Titanic, which struck an iceberg off Newfoundland on Sunday night, sank on Monday morning between Sable Island and Cape Race, in water 2 miles deep.

A Halifax message states that all the passengers had left the vessel by 3 o'clock on Monday morning. The SS Carpathia, now on her way to New York, picked up lifeboats containing 866 of the Titanic's passengers. The latter, who are mostly women, include Mrs Jacob Astor, the Countess of Rothes, Mr J B Ismay (managing director of the White Star Line), Sir Cosmo Gordon, and Mr Bahr (the well-known tennis player).

The officials of the White Star Line believe that 1,500 of the Titanic's passengers have been drowned, this estimate being based upon the number on board the SS Carpathia, to which the SS Virginia transferred those she had rescued.

The details of the disaster and of the rescue operations are, however, meagre and contradictory. The SS Parisian also went to the assistance of the Titanic, but no report has been received as to whether or not she picked up any of the passengers.

The lost vessel cost £1,250,000, and her hull and cargo were insured for £2,350,000. Reinsurances were effected on Monday at 50 guineas per cent. The liner carried £1,000,000 worth of diamonds and £500,000 worth of pearls.

Various liners recently encountered an ice field 100 miles long and 35 miles broad off the Newfoundland Grand Banks. The liner Niagara was twice holed through contact with the ice and other vessels were also damaged.

Veteran Atlantic voyagers' state that they have never before seen ice in such great bulk so far south as it is at present in the North Atlantic. The bergs are mostly without tops. They are merely awash, and it is difficult to discern them.

The New York Times for 19 April 1912 reported on the arrival of SS *Carpathia* in the harbour, under the heading 'New York Excited and Sympathetic'.

The Cunard Liner, Carpathia, arrived here at 8.30 o'clock last evening [Thursday], with 745 survivors from the ill-fated While Star liner Titanic. Interest in the arrival of the vessel was intense. Never in its history was the city so terribly impressed. Notwithstanding the rain, enormous crowds awaited the arrival of the Carpathia. A thousand relatives and friends of the survivors were permitted to go on the pier. The docking of the Carpathia was delayed while 13 lifeboats of the Titanic were lowered.

Another mystery came about when the lifeboats eventually vanished and were never seen intact again. However, among the new measures brought in after the disaster was that all ships should have enough lifeboats, so it is likely that they were transferred to *Titanic*'s sister ship, RMS *Olympic*, and several '*Titanic*' nameplates are known to be in existence. Number 5 plate is at Fairford in Gloucestershire.

In a report for *The Times* dated 21 April 1912, Bruce Ismay stated, 'In building *Titanic* it was the hope of my associates and me that we had built a vessel which could not be destroyed by the perils of the sea or dangers of navigation. The event has proved the Futility of that hope.'

One of the more descriptive accounts by a passenger concerning the disaster came from Joseph Hyman, who had been in bed for over two hours when he felt the jolt:

My stateroom was in the third class cabin, well forward, and about two decks down from the top deck. Sunday night I sat chatting with several other passengers and went to bed a few minutes after ten o'clock. It must have been about half-past-eleven when I was awakened by a terrible shock. There was only one – just a bang and a rip – lasting a couple of seconds. Then everything was quiet. I didn't know what had happened, but never dreamed it could be anything serious, so lay in my bunk for twenty minutes listening. I could hear doors banging and passengers running to and fro asking what was the matter. Someone said everything was all right, but some were afraid.

Then I got up and dressed and went out into the passage. A steward standing there told me roughly to go to the back of the ship, and I walked along the passage which ran the whole length of the vessel. On the way I passed a group of engineers and stokers, laughing, chatting and smoking cigarettes. I reached the after third class cabin, then I climbed up to the top deck, where I stood fully twenty minutes. I knew the ship had hit something, but I didn't think it could be anything serious – I don't believe anybody on board suspected anything serious.

All around me were passengers putting on life belts. Some of the women were a little frightened, but most were calm, and I thought the life belts were just an extra precaution. I looked for one but couldn't find one. There were several back in my room, but I never thought to bring one along. I saw several people climbing up the stairs which led to a sort of house on the deck just in front of me, and I thought I would see what the matter up there was. I asked several officers if there was any danger, and they said 'No, no; just keep calm.'

I climbed up the stairs, and there were a lot of men and women standing about a lifeboat. The women were being helped in, but the men didn't seem to want to get in. Then I noticed that it was the next to the last boat in that part of the ship. The others were all lowered, and I got a little uneasy. I climbed up onto the rail, and watching my chance, slipped into the boat just before they began to lower away. Most of the men thought they would be safer back on the boat, and some of them smiled at us as we went down.

The forward deck was jammed with people, all of them pushing, and clawing and fighting, and so I walked forward and stepped over the end of the boat that was being got ready and sat down [Collapsible lifeboat C, at about 1.40am]. Nobody disturbed me, and then a line of men gathered along the side and only opened when a woman or a child came forward. When a man tried to get through he would be pushed back.

There was not much panic before we left, except when the chief officer fired into a belligerent group of third class passengers. A man standing next to him had his chin shot off.

More than one hundred passengers who found seats in lifeboats were drowned when the boats struck the water and capsized. One boat, containing fifty persons, lowered down the side of the great vessel, but before it reached the water the stern tackle caught and the boat struck the water bow first, throwing the shrieking passengers, mostly women, into the water.

Among the third class passengers the confidence in the strength of *Titanic* was so great that even when the officers began to fill the lifeboats there was no panic. The terror did not begin until the lurch of the vessel showed that it was sinking. Then came two explosions. The last of which blew hundreds of persons off into the sea, maiming them and making their fight for life impossible. From the time the lights went out until the vessel plunged head first into the icy sea, there was one prolonged cry as of a single, mighty animal in mortal agony.

When we were nearly to the water we passed a big hole in the side of the boat. This was about three quarters of the way back toward the stern and the pumps were throwing a great stream of water out through it. It threatened to swamp our boat, and we got scared. There were about ten men in the boat and we each took an oar and pushed the boat away from the side of the ship. That's all that saved us.

When we settled into the water we pulled away like mad, because we didn't know whether the *Titanic* would sink or not and were afraid of the suction. When we were about fifty yards away I noticed that the portholes forward were lower than those aft, and then got my first impression that the ship was sinking. When we had pulled further away I saw the iceberg. It was black and was about fifty yards astern.

We pulled away about half a mile and then rested and watched. One by one I saw the forward portholes go out, just like someone was walking back through the ship and turning out the electric lights. Then we heard a small explosion and a terrible cry. The cry was blood curdling and never stopped until the Titanic went down, when it seemed to be sort of choked off. The cry is ringing in my ears now and always will. We sat there silent, we were terror stricken.

In less than ten minutes there came an explosion, and I could see men, women and pieces of the ship blown into the air from the after deck. I saw bodies partly blown to pieces floating around, and I am sure more than a hundred persons were blown off into the sea by that explosion. I met one man on the Carpathia who was blown off, but caught a piece of a table and floated.

At the second explosion the lights went out. Even the lights on the masthead went out. And everything was dark for a few moments. A terrible hissing of steam began and the awful cry went on. I tried to close my ears, but there was some mysterious attraction and I had to hear that cry.

When my eyes got used to the dark I could make out the Titanic, still with the front part down in the water. That was about half-past one, I guess. The hissing and screaming kept up, and finally the ship seemed to right itself, then suddenly the front end plunged down and she sank like a stone. The cry was choked off, and the hissing of steam stopped, but the sudden silence was almost more terrifying than the screams. We didn't feel the suction, except for a big wave that rocked our boat about two minutes after.

After the lifeboat in which we left *Titanic* put out some distance, shrill cries and screams could be heard distinctly.

The women were crying, but the men in our boat were still. We rowed about for a while to try and find the other boats and finally came upon four more. We also found a lot of men floating around on tables and chairs but had no room to pick up any of them. One man had tied three deck chairs together and was floating all night.

Some of the men in our boat took off their coats and threw them around the women, who were almost frozen. The wind began to blow sharply, and the boat started rocking a little, but the sea was never dangerous.

In about two hours we saw a glint of light off to the west. We watched it for an hour, and then we could see that there were two lights and it must be a ship, so we rowed toward it. The exercise kept us men warm, but the women, most of them first cabin passengers, were nearly frozen to death.

I don't recall being afraid, I remember the pleasure, really, of going plop! into the lifeboat. We ended up next to the daughter of an American banker who managed to save her dog – no one objected. There were vast differences of people's wealth on the ship, and I realized later that if we hadn't been in second-class, we'd have died. The people who came out alive often cheated and were aggressive. The honest didn't stand a chance.

We did not see the Carpathia until just before the sun was rising. With regard to the treatment of survivors on the Carpathia, it was mentioned that the stewardesses had to sleep on deck as there was no other accommodation for them, but some of the passengers of the Carpathia came out of their own rooms to enable the Titanic passengers to have use of their rooms.

As soon as it got light we could see that the ship was the Carpathia, and we reached it in another hour. We had to be lifted aboard, as some of the women were unconscious. They gave us coffee and brandy and we felt better.

After I was taken aboard the Carpathia, one capsized boat, with a steward riding astride the keel, was picked up, and the steward confirmed what I had seen. Three empty boats were picked up, riding right side up, but empty.

There were boats coming towards the Carpathia from all sides; in some were men and women badly mangled. They had to be lifted aboard on stretchers, and if it hadn't been so calm they could never have gotten aboard at all.

Carpathia stood by for four hours; then another ship came up. I don't know the name of it. They signalled to each other, and then began to take a big circle, one on each side. The circle was about twenty miles across and in the middle was a big ice floe, fully ten miles wide, but I don't think it was the one the Titanic struck. We picked up altogether sixteen boats; besides those we found three empty ones, and one had been capsized, with a man floating on top.

Carpathia then came back to where the Titanic sank. You could tell the place by the corks, boxes, bottles, chairs and things floating around on the water, and now and then a big cloud of bubbles would come up. Then we turned and made for New York.

Admiral, Lord Charles William de la Poer Beresford (1846–1919), a former Member of Parliament and Lord of the Admiralty, who was an acquaintance of Lord William Pirrie, as members of the Carlton Club in London, wrote a letter to *The Times* on 22 April 1912, in which he paid tribute to Captain Smith and the below-deck crew of *Titanic*:

> Sir – in the late appalling disaster to the Titanic, perhaps the greatest in marine history, attention has rightly been called to the bravery, resolution, and chivalrous gallantry of Captain Smith, the officers, seamen, band and passengers, who were true to the spirit of manly duty of the English-speaking races in a sudden and terrible emergency.
>
> Many comments have justly been made regarding the heroism on deck, but nothing has been said of the heroism below.
>
> I respectfully submit that, unintentionally, the dauntless heroism of those employed in the engine and boiler room departments such as the carpenter and his crew have been passed over without comment.
>
> Nothing can exceed the heroism of the captain, officers and seamen of the ship, but officers and seamen are the first to offer a whole-hearted tribute of unbounded admiration to those working below as they well know how often the real grit and courage of the officers and men of these departments is called upon in moments of emergency.
>
> It is stated that the lights were burning until a few minutes before the ship took her last plunge. This proves that the officers and men below remained at their posts when they must have known that a death – the most terrible and painful that it is possible to conceive – awaited them at any minute, either by the bursting of a steam pipe or water rising in a compartment.
>
> It is certain that those working below must have known the awful danger the ship was in long before anybody else but they remained at their posts, resolving to die sooner than come on deck to create a panic or attempt to save them.
>
> Those below must have heard the muffled sound of the ice tearing through the ship's side.
>
> Within ten minutes, or a little more, they knew that the pumps would not check the rising water, yet for over two hours they remained at their posts, as was evidence by the lights burning and the few of them who were saved by being picked-up after the ship went down.
>
> That so many people were saved was due to the fact that those working below remained at their post working the dynamos and kept the lights burning and never came on deck to state what had really happened.

Again and again the indomitable pluck and discipline of those who work below in the engine and boiler rooms is illustrated when some terrible disaster of the sea occurs, but on no occasion have these traits been more brilliantly shown.

It should be remembered that those below work in confined spaces, water-tight doors closed, often in intolerable heat, with roar of machinery making orders difficult to understand.

A man will face death with greater equanimity on deck than working below under the incidents I have mentioned. Working below really requires more fortitude and pluck.

All honour and respect to those men whose names will be recorded on the roll of fame for gallantry in a sudden and unlooked for disaster. But I am sure the survivors of this shocking catastrophe will serve with me in placing those who worked below in 'The right of the line'.

It is interesting to note that Admiral Beresford's family, some of whom were the Marquesses of Waterford, suffered a number of misfortunes that led them to believe they were the victims of a malevolent curse. Henry, the 3rd Marquess, was killed in 1859 when he was thrown from a horse and broke his neck. John Henry, the 5th Marquess, shot himself in 1895, having been worn down by years of suffering after a crippling hunting accident. His son, Henry, the 6th Marquess, after having narrowly escaped being mauled to death by a lion while big game hunting in Africa, drowned in a river on his estate in 1911; aged only 36. The 7th Marquess was killed in a shooting accident in the gun room at the family home of Curraghmore in Ireland; aged only 33. Lord William Beresford, who had gained the award of Victoria Cross during the Zulu War of 1879, fell from a horse in 1900 and received injuries from which he never recovered; and his brother, Delaval, became a rancher in North America and was killed in a railway accident in Texas in 1906.

An abridged version of Lord Mersey's report on the loss of *Titanic* appeared in British newspapers on 2 August 2012:

Lord Mersey attributed the chief cause of the disaster to the excessive speed at which the ship was being driven, but he does not blame Captain Smith, because in driving the Titanic so fast through an ice region, and trusting solely to the lookout, he was only doing what other masters had done for years, and would have done had they been in his place, because they believed it could be done with impunity. It had been shown in evidence that for a quarter of a century or more the practice of liners using the same track, when in the vicinity of ice at night, had been in clear weather to keep the course, to maintain the speed, and to trust to a sharp look-out to enable them to avoid the danger. This practice, it was said, had been justified by experience, no casualties having resulted from it.'

Lord Mersey observed: 'But the event has proved the practice to be bad. Its root is probably to be found in competition and the desire of the public for quick passages, rather than in the judgment of navigators. Unfortunately experience appeared to justify it. In this circumstance, I am not able to blame Captain Smith. He had not the experience which his own misfortune has afforded to those he has left behind; and he was only doing that which other skilled men would have done in the same position.'

The evidence shows that he [Captain Smith] was not trying to make any record passage, or, indeed, exceptionally quick passage. He was not trying to please anybody, but was exercising his own discretion in the way he thought best. He made a mistake, a very grievous mistake, but one in which, in face of past experience, negligence cannot be said to have had any part. However, what was a mistake in the case of the Titanic would without doubt be negligence in any similar case in the future.

The cause of the Titanic's sinking was due to the vessel being damaged for a length of 300 feet, so that no less than six watertight compartments were open to the sea at a point about 10 feet above the keel.

Referring to the attack made on Sir C Duff Gordon, Lord Mersey says, 'The very gross charge of having got into No. 1 boat, and that he bribed the men in it to row away from drowning people is unfounded. At the same time, I think that if he had encouraged the men to return to the position where the Titanic foundered they would probably have made an effort to do so, and could have saved some lives.

As to the attack on Mr Ismay, the report says that the suggestion was that in occupying the position of managing director of the steamship company, some moral duty was imposed on him to wait on board until the vessel foundered. I do not agree. Mr Ismay, after rendering assistance to many passengers, found a collapsible, the last boat on the starboard side, actually being lowered. No other people were there at the time. There was room for him, and he jumped in. Had he not he would merely have added one life, namely his own, to the number of those lost.

As to whether the Californian saw Titanic, Lord Mersey simply notes that the vessel seen by the Californian stopped at 11.40 – Titanic collided at 11.40. The Californian saw eight distress signals from about 12.45 to 1.45 – Titanic sent up eight distress signals about the same time. At 2.40 the Californian's officer called to his captain that the ship had disappeared – at 2.30 Titanic had foundered.

Lord Mersey says: 'These circumstances convince me that the ship seen by the Californian was the Titanic, and if so, according to Captain Lord, the two vessels were about five miles apart. I advised that the distance was probably greater, though not more than eight to ten miles. The ice by which the Californian was surrounded was loose ice, extending for a distance of not more than two or three miles in the direction of the Titanic.

'The night was clear and the sea was smooth. When she first saw the rockets the Californian could have passed through the ice to the open water without any serious risk, and so have come to the assistance of the Titanic. Had she done so she might have saved many, if not all of the lives that were lost.'

The *Daily Telegraph*'s New York correspondent reported on 17 January 1913 on 'Titanic Claims – Total of over £1,100,000':

Amongst the claims in connection with the Titanic disaster filed here, some in respect of 'mental and physical suffering' by survivors and relations. The total amount asked is now over £1,100,000.

No claims have been submitted by Mrs John Jacob Astor, by the Wideners of Philadelphia, or by the family of Mr Charles Hays, former president of the Grand Trunk Railroad. The brother of Major Archibald Butt, military attaché to President Taft, put in a claim for the loss of his brother's personal baggage, but asked nothing for the loss of the major's life.

The largest claim is that of Mrs Irene Harris, widow of Mr Henry B Harris, the theatrical manager, for £200,000. Among Mrs Harris's losses was a pearl necklace valued at £2000. Mrs Charlotte Cardeza, of Germantown, Pennsylvania, seeks to recover £26,000 for the loss of her wardrobe and other effects. Her inventory includes a Burma ruby ring valued at £3000, a pink diamond valued at £4000, £100 worth of hatpins, and a white petticoat estimated at £20. Mrs Lilly Millet, of New York, asks £20,000 for the loss of her husband, Mr Frank Millet, the artist, who was drowned. Mrs May Frutelle, widow of Mr Jacques Frutelle, the author, asked £60,000 for the death of her husband. Mr Bjornstrom Stefansson demands £20,000 for the loss of an oil painting entitled 'The Circassia at the Bath,' and valued his personal baggage at £500. Mrs Catherine Horbeck, widow of Mr William Horbeck, asked £5000 for her husband's life and £11,000 for the loss of 110,000 feet of moving picture films. In the case of the Skoogh family, where the mother, father, and four children went down, £30,000 was demanded by the old grandfather and grandmother in Europe. Among the claims of many honeymoon couples is that of Mrs Adele Nasrallah of Brooklyn. She is the mother of the third Titanic baby. Mrs Nasrallah asks £10,000 for the loss of her husband and £2000 for that of her baggage and jewellery.

These are samples of the claims I have selected from a long list. There is an amazing difference in the assessments of the value of husbands, the amounts ranging from a modest £100 to Mrs Harris's £200,000. So far as one can gauge at present there is not a very brilliant prospect of compelling the Ocean Steam Navigation Company to pay more than a nominal sum, and many people have not even taken the trouble to present a claim, except in omnibus form.

The RMS *Titanic* disaster is one of history's most catastrophic human tragedies, which resulted in a terrible sacrifice of life. The people on board were proud to be part of the ship's maiden voyage, but what they didn't know was that it was destined to be its only voyage. It harbours many heartbreaking stories about its ill-fated passengers and crew, whose lives were painfully shattered by what they saw and experienced during that one dreadful incident.

2. PRECOGNITIONS

The well-known newspaper editor William Thomas Stead, a keen believer in spiritualism, had accepted an all-expenses-paid invitation from President William Howard Taft (1857–1930) to speak on world peace at the next congress of the Men and Religion Forward Movement, at Carnegie Hall in New York on 21 April 1912. He booked tickets on *Titanic* for the journey and lost his life in the disaster. On 22 March 1886, he had published an article in the *Pall Mall Gazette*, entitled 'How the Mail Steamer went down in mid-Atlantic, by a Survivor' (see Appendix IV).

The plot of the story follows a British sailor called Thomas who goes to work on a newly built passenger liner that embarks on its maiden voyage to the United States. Thomas realises that the number of lifeboats on board are not enough to save all the passengers and crew, and although he expresses his concerns, his warnings are ignored A few days into the journey the liner collides with a stray sailing ship, which had not been visible due to thick fog. In the panic that follows, the people on board realise that Thomas was correct and there are far too few lifeboats. Of the 916 on board, only about 200 manage to get in lifeboats, including Thomas, but more than 700 souls lose their lives. Stead concluded: 'This is exactly what might take place and will take place if liners are sent to sea short of boats – Ed.'

The White Star Line constructed a ship named *Majestic* and it was launched in 1889, and three years later in the Christmas 1892 edition of Stead's magazine *Review of Reviews* he told the story entitled 'From the Old World to the New: Or, A Christmas Story of the Chicago Exhibition'. It is about a ship named *Majestic* of the White Star Line, which has set sail from Liverpool to the 1893 Chicago World Fair with a clairvoyant named Mrs Irwin on board, who second-sights a disaster to another ship that has collided with an iceberg. The survivors are rescued and the *Majestic* manages to avoid the ice.

Also in 1891 and 1892, Stead published a collection of psychic experience stories that he called *Real Ghost Stories*. One of these stories is about a member of the crew of the sailing ship *Persian Empire* who has a precognition dream, the consequences of ignoring it, and a sister's vision.

Persian Empire left Adelaide in Australia bound for London in September 1868, with a Mr Fleet serving as third mate. Mr Fleet befriended another member of the crew by the name of Cleary, who told him about a dream he had before *Persian Empire* left Adelaide. He dreamed that as the ship passed Cape Horn in a heavy storm, the captain ordered Cleary and the rest of his watch to secure a boat which was hanging in davits over the side of the ship. Cleary and another crew member got into the boat. Then a mountainous sea rolled in, washing both men out of the boat into the sea and they drowned. The dream made such a vivid impression on Cleary that he almost didn't join *Persian Empire*'s crew, but in the end he signed up and sailed with her.

On 25 December 1868, Mr Cleary's dream became a reality. The chief officer ordered him and the rest of the watch to secure a boat hanging in the davits. Mr Cleary refused because he knew that if he went into that boat he would die. The mate took Mr Cleary below to the captain and the captain entered his refusal to perform a duty in the log. Then the chief officer, Douglas, picked up the pen to sign his name. Cleary looked at him and exclaimed, 'I will go to my duty for now I know the other man in my dream.'

Cleary and Douglas got into the boat and when they were making tight a heavy wave struck the boat, overturned it, and Douglas and Cleary were thrown into the ocean. Three months after Cleary had dreamed his terrible dream before leaving Adelaide, it had come true.

A great gust of wind seized the half-slackened main top sail of *Persian Empire* and the ship rolled nearly on her beam. Above the howling of the wind, third mate Fleet heard a cry of despair. He watched in horror as apprentice seaman Joe P plunged headlong from the mast-head into the sea, crying out the name Lucy as he sank under the waves.

As soon as *Persian Empire* arrived in Liverpool, third mate Fleet hurried to the train that would take him to Manchester. He was walking along the platform when he spotted an old gentleman with a young lady on his arm elbowing his way through the crowd. The old gentleman looked so much like the lost seaman Joe P that third mate Fleet stared at him, and the young woman stared back at him, calling out, 'Oh look, there's the face of my dream!'

The old gentleman helped her to the nearest waiting room, beckoning third mate Fleet to follow him. He explained that Fleet's face had reminded his daughter of a constant, disturbing dream that was haunting her. He said that they were on their way to find out if the owners of his son's ship had received any news of its arrival.

Fleet told them that he was a third mate on *Persian Empire* and had just left her. The young woman cried that she had seen her brother Joe's ship in the middle of a terrible storm and she had seen him clinging to the slippery sails. She said, 'A bright flash seemed to pass before my eyes, and I saw him falling backwards into the sea. I saw your face in the momentary gleam, and I woke perfectly terrified to hear the sound of my own name, 'Oh Lucy! Lucy!' whispered in my ears.

Fleet told the old gentleman that his daughter's dream was true. They compared notes and found that his daughter had dreamed the very day, and allowing for the difference in longitude, the very hour of her brother's death.

Stead also told of a dream he had in which he saw himself standing on the deck of a rapidly sinking ocean liner, without a lifebelt, and with the last lifeboat vanishing into the night. But Stead, a man who obviously believed in fate, ignored all the omens and booked his ticket on *Titanic*.

***

It would seem that an American short story writer called Morgan Andrew Robertson had some form of preconception of the disaster fourteen years before it happened.

In 1898 he published a book entitled *Futility*, about a fictional ocean liner called *Titan*, which sank after hitting an iceberg and does not carry enough lifeboats for everyone on board. *Titan* and *Titanic* were roughly the same size, and they both sank 400 nautical miles from Newfoundland on an April evening. Although the fact and fictional similarities are uncanny, Robertson later stated that he did not have any psychic abilities, as his novel was based on his knowledge of shipbuilding and his understanding of the dangers of modern shipping.

It was reissued in 1912 after the *Titanic* sank, under the title *The Wreck of the Titan*. He made some updates to the new version, including increasing the dimensions and power of *Titan* to try to match those of the *Titanic*, without making it too obvious that he was attempting to cash in on the tragedy. Robertson gained quite a reputation for being a clairvoyant, which he always denied, simply stating: 'I know what I am writing about, that's all!' – And in that comment lies the answer.

***

At the time of the sinking of *Titanic* the May issue of the *Popular Magazine* was already on the news stands. It included a short story by Captain Mayn Clew Garnett entitled *The White Ghost of Disaster: The Chief Mate's Yarn*. It was about an ocean liner that strikes an iceberg in the Atlantic Ocean and sinks. One of the main characters is called Smith. The story caused a minor sensation, and many people attributed to Garnett the gift of foresight. However, his chequered past had caused him to have to use a pseudonym, his real name being Thornton Alexander Jenkins Hains (1866–1953). The son of a United States Army general and veteran of the Civil War, he was a writer on seafaring life, who was acquitted of killing a man by shooting him in 1891, and in August 1908 of being an accessory to a murder committed by his brother, Peter, who killed his wife's lover.

***

From 9 January to 24 April 1912 the German *Berliner Tageblatt* newspaper published a story in serial form that was written by Gerhart Hauptmann (1862–1946), who received the Nobel Prize for Literature later that year. One month before the *Titanic* disaster it was published as a novel entitled 'Atlantis'; a romantic story set aboard the fictitious liner *Roland*, which was doomed to a fate very similar to that of *Titanic*. This anticipation of the disaster received considerable attention at the time. A Danish silent film, also entitled *Atlantis* and based on the novel, was released less than a year after the tragic event. The obvious association with the disaster and the novel was considered to be in bad taste and was not well received.

***

Titanic was not the first British ship to sink during its maiden voyage. Of the many previous incidents, one concerned RMS *Tayleur*, often described as 'The First Titanic'. Constructed in just six months at the Bank Quay Foundry in Warrington for Charles Moore and Company, and chartered for the White Star Line, she was a full-rigged iron clipper emigrant ship of nearly 2,000 tons chartered for the Australian trade routes. Launched on 4 October 1853, she left the River Mersey in Liverpool bound for Melbourne in Australia for her maiden voyage on 19 January 1854.

The crew believed they were sailing southward through the Irish Sea, when they were actually travelling westward towards Ireland. It was later discovered that the ship's compass had not worked properly due to the ship's iron hull, so she had headed straight for the isle of Lambay, a few miles north of the fishing village of Howth, which

18

forms the northern boundary of the bay of Dublin. To add to her peril, on 21 January a storm arose, and she became caught in thick fog.

When the fog lifted they became aware that they were too close to reefs, so two anchors were dropped, but their chains snapped and the ship continued to drift towards the shore, where it struck on the rocks. It was considered to be too dangerous to launch the lifeboats, so some of the crew collapsed a mast onto the shore so that the passengers could use it as a means of escape by clambering along it. Some of them had carried ropes from the ship, which they then used to pull others to relative safety. The ship's 29-year-old captain, John Noble, stayed on board until the last minute, then he jumped towards the shore, being helped to safety by one of the passengers. The ship was completely consumed by the sea, leaving just the top of her mast showing.

After being alerted by a survivor, the coast guard made their way to the wreck, where they encountered the last survivor, a man named William Vivers, who had managed to climb to the top of the exposed rigging, where he clung on for fourteen hours waiting to be rescued. Of the 572 passengers and crew who had been on board the vessel only 280 survived, and of over 200 women only three were saved.

On 2 March 1854, the chief lifeboatman, George Finlay, was awarded the Royal National Lifeboat Institution's silver medal for his part in the rescue. The citation reads:

> On 21 January 1854, the 1,997 ton emigrant sailing ship 'Tayleur' left Liverpool for Australia on 19 January 1854, with 71 crew and 501 passengers, many of them bound for the goldfields.
>
> As soon as she entered the Irish Sea she encountered rough weather which worsened during the night, and the fog became so thick next morning, that observations could not be taken. The combination of inaccurate navigation and an unsatisfactory crew meant that at 11:30am on the 21st she was found to be on a dead lee shore with bad visibility. The vessel dropped two anchors to try to ride out the south to south-westerly gale, but both cables snapped immediately and the ship drifted on the rocks at the east point of Lambay Island, off Howth Head.
>
> Because of the broken water the lifeboats could not be launched; a passenger then swam ashore with a line and clinging to this, a number of people were saved, although many drowned in the attempt.
>
> A heavy sea washed the ship back and she sank in deep water taking with her 270 people, but one was seen to be still in the rigging from where he was rescued by the coastguard galley, which had been launched by Mr Finlay, three coastguards and a rescued passenger.

***

There were numerous incidents recorded during the nineteenth century where ships had sunk after hitting an iceberg, and it is interesting to note that there were several ships with a similar name to *Titanic* and *Titan* – namely *Titania* – which were involved in incidents on the high seas, and the name was well-known for being given to ships throughout the Victorian era.

1882 – Built at the Sir Raylton Dixon and Company shipyard in Middlesbrough, and launched in 1880, the British iron brig cargo ship SS *Titania* struck an iceberg on 25 January 1882 while sailing through fog about 50 miles south-east of the headland of Cape Spear, on its voyage from St John's in Newfoundland to Miramichi in New Brunswick, Canada. She sank after three hours.

1886 – A ship built by Mounsey and Foster in Sunderland in 1879, and originally named SS *Mercedes*, was sold to a German company in 1886, and renamed SS *Titania*. It was sold to the United States Navy in 1898 and used as a collier supply ship with the name SS *Marcellus*.

1894 – On 15 April 1894, a very well-publicised incident that made news all around the world occurred when SS *Titania* collided with SS *Koroowarra*.

1896 – A new cargo ship named SS *Titania* was launched at the Low Walker Shipyard on the Tyne on 24 April 1896, being destined for service from Helsinki.

1897 – In late July 1897, the same SS *Titania* that collided with SS *Koroowarra* was in the North Atlantic on a voyage from Dalhousie in New Brunswick, Canada, to Glasgow, with a cargo of timber. The ship began to sink, and although the eleven-man crew tried to pump the water out of the vessel for four days, she sank on 3 August 1897. The ship had originally been built at the St Lawrence Yard in Newcastle, and launched on 5 January 1852 for the India trade.

The *Launceston Examiner* for 19 October 1897 reported in its 'Shipping Casualties' column: 'News has been received of the total loss of the bark Titania which was built in 1852 at Newcastle, England. The vessel was abandoned in a sinking condition by the crew in 46.23 N. and 44.30 W, on 3 August 1897. The crew was subsequently picked up by the Russian bark Vega, which landed the men at Swansea. The Titania had been sinking gradually for four days, during which the crew was constantly pumping. The shipwrecked men, 11 in number, were in a much exhausted state when rescued. They were off Newfoundland when the Vega hove in sight of them and took them aboard. The Titania was bound to Glasgow.'

***

The *Vancouver Daily Province* for 2 May 1912, records that at Suva, the capital city of the Fiji Islands, on (or after) 16 April 1912, the officers of the liner *Marama* were told by the inhabitants that *Titanic* had gone down with heavy loss of life. Two days after their departure for Honolulu, *Marama* received a wireless message saying that *Titanic* had struck an iceberg, but was being towed to safety. The officers could not explain how Fiji knew about *Titanic's* loss two days before the first reports of the collision reached this area of the Pacific.

This may have something to do with time zones. Also, news of *Titanic's* sinking was published in British and American newspapers before the end of the day on Tuesday, 16 April 1912. The Fijians could have received the news not long afterwards, and not two days later as stated. Two important questions have, and will probably never be answered – when exactly did news of the disaster reach Fiji? And where was SS *Marama* when it received the news?

The Pacific cable line had already been in use in Fiji for a decade, as the *Melbourne Leader* for 12 April 1902, recorded:

Fiji is now in communication with the outside world by cable. Yesterday the postmaster-general received a telegram to the following effect from the Brisbane opened with Fiji via the Pacific cable at 6pm today (Thursday), and congratulatory messages addressed to London and to the governor-general were received from the administrator there. Mr Drake has cabled to the administrators of the Islands as follows – 'Hearty congratulations on the auspicious occasion of the establishment of telegraphic communication by means of the Pacific cable between Fiji, Australia, the British Empire, and the countries of the world generally. Trust it will tend to the mutual prosperity of Fiji and Australia.

It is announced that the portion of the Pacific cable now complete – that portion lying between Australia, New Zealand, Norfolk Island and Fiji, will open for the public within a few weeks.

The SS *Marama* was an ocean liner built by Caird and Company at Greenock in Scotland, and launched in 1907. It was the largest and most powerful ship in the USS Company fleet at that time. It saw service with the Union Company of New Zealand from 1907 to 1937, and initially sailed on the Horseshoe Run between New Zealand and Australia, and some trans-Pacific services. It was adopted as a hospital ship during the Great War, and was broken up in 1937.

3. CURSES

The White Star Line did not observe the tradition of christening their boats, with many people believing that such a practice was a bad omen, and that to call the liner 'unsinkable' was flying in the face of God (See Appendix III).

A young lad named John Parkinson watched with emotion as the great liner was launched on 31 May 1911, because Frank, his father, had worked on the ship. He said to his dad: 'How can a ship that big stay on the water?' to which Frank replied confidently: 'Johnny, that ship will always stay up in the water!'

While all the pomp and circumstance of the day was being recorded, James Dobbin, a 43-year-old shipwright, was responsible for looking after the giant chains and wooden props that held *Titanic* secure on the slipway. As the great ship moved and the greased stanchions that had been helping to keep her in place fell away, James was completely unaware that one of them was falling his way, or he did not have a chance to get out of the way when he realised the danger, and he was crushed to death as a mass of heavy timbers piled on top of him.

James was the fourth of eight men who lost their lives during the construction of RMS *Titanic*, the names of three of them having never been recorded, and one of them had already lost his son during the construction of RMS *Olympic*. However, it was considered to be a low casualty count in comparison to the vast labour force employed at the yard, the massive scope of the project, and the almost non-existent safety regulations. Harland and Wolff issued a report on 10 April 1912 (the day *Titanic* left Southampton) listing the casualties connected with the construction and fitting out of the two ships. *Olympic* was stated as nine fatal, fourteen severe and 206 slight accidents. *Titanic* had eight fatal, twenty-eight severe and 218 slight accidents – a total of 483 accidents for the two liners.

***

Esther Hart (1863–1928), her husband, Benjamin (1864–1912), and their 7-year-old daughter Eva Miriam (1905–96), had travelled down to Southampton from Essex on the boat train. They were originally booked on SS *Philadelphia*, but Ben changed his plans because he wanted to visit a relative in New York while he had the chance and therefore they transferred to *Titanic*. Esther had never had any kind of premonitions before, but she considered all the talk of the ship being unsinkable was flying in the face of God, and she stated: 'I can honestly say that from the moment the journey to Canada was mentioned till the time we got aboard *Titanic* I never contemplated with any other feelings but those of dread and uneasiness.'

Edith Louise Rosenbaum (1879–1975), later known as Edith Russell, was a 33-year-old first-class passenger. She was the daughter of a clothes manufacturer, who was travelling on *Titanic* after reporting on fashion at the Paris Easter Sunday Races, and had boarded the ship at Cherbourg. She had tried to get insurance for her numerous amounts of luggage – and small toy musical pig – but was told that insurance was not necessary because the ship was unsinkable.

She posted a letter to her secretary at Queenstown, in which she praised the liner as 'the most wonderful boat you could think of . . .' but also remarked that, 'I'm going to take my very much needed rest on this trip, but I cannot get over my feeling of depression and premonition of trouble. How I wish it was over!'

Albert and Sylvia Caldwell had been working at the Bangkok Christian College in Siam (now Thailand) and they were on their way back to their home in Illinois with their baby, Alden. As they were waiting to board *Titanic*, Sylvia watched a group of deckhands carrying luggage aboard. She spontaneously asked one of the men 'Is this ship really unsinkable?'

'Yes', he replied, 'God himself couldn't sink this ship.'

***

On Friday night, 12 April 1912, several passengers on *Titanic* were enjoying a dinner party, as the liner pushed on through the waves. Among them was W T Stead. Stories had been in newspapers recently concerning the lid of a sarcophagus in the British Museum, which had once contained the mummy of the sun priestess Amen-Ra. It came to be known as the 'Unlucky Mummy', as misfortune came to almost everyone who came into contact with it and there were dozens of stories circulating about it. Also at the table was Frederic Kimber Seward, who gave an interview with the *New York World* a few days after the disaster in which he stated that Stead related stories about the mummy to his fascinated table companions, which he said lasted until after midnight.

It is believed this story began rumours that the mummy of Tcheser-Ka-Ra, the High Priestess Amen-Ra of Thebes, was on *Titanic*. However, although there was no actual mummy on the ship, and a lid of the sarcophagus that is said to have once contained the Amen-Ra mummy can be seen in the Egyptian Room at the British Museum – is it possible that an Egyptian artefact was on the ship?

In *His Five Decades of Adventure* (volume 2), published in 1920, Frederic Villiers (1851-1922), the well-known Victorian war artist and correspondent, stated that he was with Lt Walter Ingram in a 'mummy shop' at Wadi Halfa in the Sudan when Ingram bought the coffin of a mummy. When opened 'there was a long papyrus on his breast setting forth a horrible curse. It threatens anyone who disturbs his long rest in his sarcophagus with a violent death, and predicts that the bones of the culprit will be swept to the seas or scattered to the winds.' – thus being deprived of a decent burial. Ingram was trampled to death by a rogue elephant in Somaliland in 1888, and there was a legend that his bones were washed away by heavy rains into the sea.

Villiers stated: 'Whoever came in actual contact with that mummy after it left its home in Egypt suffered in some way or other. What became of that mummy case I don't know, more than that it eventually found its way into the cellars of the British Museum in London. I heard in one of the clubs in New York in 1919 that it had been sold to an American who didn't care a row about these Old World legends, and that while he was bringing it to the New World it went down with its owner in the ill-fated *Titanic*.'

It is a dreadfully long list of people who suffered great misfortune when associated with the Amen-Ra coffin lid, and it is interesting to include some examples here. The *London Express* for 3 August 1904, reported under the headline 'A Mummy Mystery – Curse of the Priestess of Amen-Ra':

The strange mystery surrounding the coffin of the Priestess of Amen-Ra, which is getting such an unenviable reputation in the Egyptian room of the British Museum, has aroused widespread interest. Many letters have reached The *London Express* office from readers who either express their scepticism or add new data to the growing list.

One letter from a professional man is a remarkable document. It tells how a year ago, having some time to spare, he wandered into that fatal Egyptian room and stood face to face with the malignant priestess, whom he likened to a suffragist. Next morning he was discharged from his occupation, and has done nothing since.

But this is not the worst. His son, previously a bright, clever boy, who carried every prize before him, became ill, and has since developed suicidal mania, which necessitated his conveyance to an asylum. On top of this comes the news of an absconding secretary of a building society, who has disappeared with the last of this unfortunate man's savings.

Among the letters received are the following: 'With reference to our article on the Priestess of Amen-Ra, I should like to add to the list of misfortunes those of three friends of mine, who each had in their possession an illustrated account of the mystery of the mummy. One was nearly run over and slightly injured; another had a fall and internal injuries; the third also had a fall resulting in the loss of a tooth, and two chimneys fell on the house she occupied.

J. M. W. Sir – It may interest you to hear of another misfortune to one, or rather two, who have been interested in the British Museum mummy. Having heard much of this mysterious mummy, one day in April (the 21st) I took the opportunity of visiting the Museum in the company of my friend, with the idea of making an investigation of this mummy case. I was unable to obtain any further information from the attendants in the room than that already published, but I felt convinced that there was something behind mere rumours that hover about this case.

Now, within a few weeks of our 'interview' my friend lost his position, and I followed a few weeks later, and neither of us has been able to obtain another position, and with a family to keep and the last few pounds going rapidly, the prospect is anything but assuring. I was manager of a large machinery firm – interested . . .

The *Occult Review* for 20 February 1913, reported:

A party of ladies visited the Museum in order to see the mummy case. Among them was a young lady belonging to a distinguished family well known in the world of fashion and in politics. She danced in front of the mummy and made grimaces at it, defying it to do its worst. In the Museum itself she met with an accident which prevented her from appearing at her own coming-out party and kept her to the house for a considerable period.

Mrs Gordon, sister of Captain Bertram Dickson, the well-known aviator, tells the following remarkable story of her own and her brother's experiences of the Priestess of Amen-Ra: Captain Bertram Dickson was staying with me on his return from the Persian frontier, where he had been as military consul at Van for four years; years packed with revolutions, political excitements, and expeditions into the unknown parts of the country, mapping and exploring. During these expeditions he had found several interesting old rings, necklaces, etc, and it was to show these to Professor Wallace Budge that we went to the British Museum.

The thought of seeing the mummy never entered our heads, and although I know all about her I had no idea that Dr Budge's office was in the same part of the building as the mummies. The attendant, however, pointed her out while we waited, and I examined her with interest and real sympathy.

Within six weeks I was badly wrecked on the Albanian coast, on a clear night, though wet, there was no storm, and yet we ran with a fearful crash which shot us out of our berths at 11.30 at night, on to the great cliffs of Ithaca.

The boats were not lowered for an hour, and indescribable confusion prevailed. Not trusting myself to them, I clambered on to the towering cliffs and hung there with some others, one leg and hands cut and bleeding and wet to the skin, till a passing steamer saw our signals of distress and picked us up at 12 o'clock next day.

My brother's case was worse. A now well-known aviator, he took it up shortly after his visit to the Museum, and at first met with great success, his pluck and skill enabling him to clear the boards at all the big French meetings.

On 1 October, while flying at the Milan meeting, another aeroplane going faster than his tried to pass over him, and at the height of 170 feet both fell crashing to the ground. The other man escaped with a scratch; my brother was terribly injured; it took them twenty minutes to dig him out of the debris, happily unconscious. While he was in hospital the bank in which all his money was deposited went smash and ruined him.

Nothing happened to any other members of the family, who did not come in contact with the mummy-case, several of whom were travelling and might have come in for adventures. One, for instance, went elephant shooting in Malay.

Two years after the *Titanic* disaster the *Globe* newspaper for 20 April 1914 reported under the headline 'Notorious Coffin Lid Not on the Titanic – Strange Statements':

A strange story appears in the *'International Psychic Gazette'* regarding the coffin lid of Amen-Ra in the British Museum, to which is attributed by some certain malevolent powers.

It is to the effect that, unknown to the public, the cover, at the urgent request of alarmed attendants, was removed some time ago to the cellars of the museum and substituted by a replica, made and painted in exact facsimile. At once complaints of the evil eye, and so on, ceased.

By-and-by, however, the story continues, an American Egyptologist inspected the coffin and ascertained that it was certainly not genuine. It was a faithful copy, but his expert eye discovered it to be a fraud!

The drop on the British Museum exhibiting a fake was an event of first-class importance, and an exposure that would have brought world-wide ridicule upon the venerable British repository of antiquarian art and treasure seemed imminent.

The curators, therefore, took the American visitor into their confidence and explained what had been done. Moreover, they took him to the cellars and showed him the original coffin, and he declared that he was satisfied. 'But look ye here,' he said, 'I guess this fine mummy case is not a bit of good to you in your cellars. I want that coffin for America! I'll make you a bid for it! He did, and it was sold to him on his own terms.

It was packed carefully, so that no one could guess what its covering-case contained; and arrangements were made that no hitch would he caused by Customs House examinations. And so the coffin was despatched to America on board Titanic. It now rests miles deep in the Atlantic. The question which is being discussed is whether the coffin's reputed diabolic power hurled the leviathan to its doom.

The story, sufficiently absurd on the face of it, would be very thrilling if it were true. But it is not. A Globe representative who made enquiries at the museum today was informed that the account in the 'International Psychic Gazette' is without foundation.

A remarkable number of communications concerning the alleged evil influence of this cover are being received by the Museum authorities from people who, after looking at it, complain that they have been stricken with physical or material woe. And the most curious part of it is that most of these correspondents attribute their misfortune to the mummy, which as a matter of fact is not in the possession of the Museum authorities.

One individual, for example, wrote that he had been seized with neuralgia and cardiac pains after looking at the cover. Yet he protested, he had thought kindly of the dead woman who had held such high office in the College of Amen-Ra at Thebes some 3,500 years ago. He was convinced that he was only being punished thus because of the lady's desire that her body should be placed in its rightful tomb, and he begged the authorities to soothe her restless spirit by carrying out her wishes.

On being informed that, unfortunately, the Museum did not possess the mummy which was supposed to have affected him, the correspondent still asserted that he was suffering because of the spirit's unhappiness.

On one occasion a party of spiritualists who were convinced that they could demonstrate the possession by the cover of some amazing powers, asked leave to be allowed to spend a night in the mummy room. The request was refused.

It must have been noticed by those who frequent this part of the museum that a photograph of the mummy cover, which formally stood at its foot and showed a remarkable expression on the face, has now been removed. This, it is stated, belonged to a private individual, and has been taken away by him.

The attribution of evil influence and power to this particular coffin lid is said to be due to its having been confused with a mummy possessed by a lady in Bayswater, which was credited with the most diabolical powers.

According to W T Stead, the meeting of spiritualists did take place in the mummy room at the British Museum. The museum tried to play down the story and avert attention away from the coffin lid for obvious reasons, and there are many examples of how items associated with Egyptology have developed into myths and mysteries, especially during the Victorian and Edwardian eras; such as the Courtoy Egyptian tomb at Brompton Cemetery in West London (see Appendix V).

However, in this case, although the commercial cargo manifest for *Titanic* does not record the presence of an Egyptian coffin lid, as the various newspaper reports explain, 'It was packed carefully, so that no one could guess what its covering case contained; and arrangements were made that no hitch would he caused by Customs House examinations.' The manifest included several cases easily large enough to contain the coffin lid, and it could have been secreted in one of the general commercial cases such as that of the American Express Company, which included '25 cases of merchandise' – the contents of which were not specified.

The case made by the British Museum that the Amen-Ra coffin lid could not have been on *Titanic* is not convincing, and the manifest does not mention a number of other Egyptian artefacts that are said to have been on the ship.

When the Denver socialite and philanthropist Mrs J J (Margaret) Brown (1867–1932), boarded *Titanic* at Cherbourg on the evening of 10 April 1912 she had with her four crates of Egyptian artefacts and souvenirs, some of which she intended to give to the Denver Museum.

Another Egyptian item not in the cases was a small figurine known as a ushabti (also known as a shabti or shawabti), which she had purchased in Cairo and kept with her as a lucky talisman, or as an exotic curio she could show off to other passengers during the trip. It was later described as being 3in tall and made from 'faience with a turquoise glaze'.

Ushabtis were placed in burial sites from the Egyptian Middle Kingdom, between about 4,000 and 3,500 years ago, until the Ptolemaic Period, around 2,500 years ago. They evolved from the belief that the afterlife would be similar to the living world. People believed they would be surrounded by friends and family even in death, and would therefore need food and drink; the Gods might even call on them to work. The ancient Egyptians hoped that a ushabti would magically do the work for them. They were servants for the afterlife.

Margaret was picked up by CS *Carpathia*, and after the rescue Captain Arthur Rostron was presented with numerous awards, including a medal that was struck by the United States Congress. However, the strangest gift came from Margaret, who presented him with her lucky talisman and this remained in his possession until his death in 1940.

She does not mention it in her descriptions of that tragic night when she escaped *Titanic* in lifeboat 6. However, according to the Molly Brown House Museum in Denver, it is known that 'she grabbed $500 in cash, strapped on a life jacket and grabbed a blanket from the bed'. The museum is also aware that Margaret and her daughter, Helen, visited Giza in Egypt.

The title 'unsinkable' was supposedly given to Molly after a press interview when she was safely on dry land in America. She put her survival down to 'Typical Brown luck'. And she added, 'We're unsinkable'; presumably meaning her and the ushabti.

Margaret Brown made a claim for just over $27,000 against the White Star Line for the loss of personal items. These included souvenirs (Egypt) – $500, and three crates of ancient models for Denver Museum – $500.

The ushabti came into the possession of an American named Stanley Lehrer, who was the founder of the *USA Today* newspaper and collected *Titanic*-related artefacts. In 1998 an exhibition called '*Titanic*: Fortune and Fate' was mounted at the Mariners' Museum at Newport News in Virginia. Lehrer was involved and a small illustration of the figurine appears in the catalogue, being described as 'An Ancient Egyptian figurine, shawabti or ushabti, circa 700BC'.

In 2006 the ushabti appeared as an item in an exhibition held at a new purpose-built permanent venue named the Titanic-Branson Museum in Branson, Missouri, which also housed a replica of *Titanic*, complete with a real iceberg, and featured '400 priceless artefacts and historical treasures'.

Dives down to *Titanic* are made regularly by manned and unmanned deep sea submersibles and artefacts from the ship are retrieved. Perhaps some time in the future the Amen-Ra coffin lid and Unsinkable Molly's artefacts will be brought to the surface.

***

George Herbert, 5th Lord Carnarvon (1866–1923), was the financial backer of the search for the excavation of Tutankhamen's tomb in the

Valley of the Kings, which was discovered by excavators led by the British archaeologist Howard Carter (1874–1939) in November 1922. When Carnarvon was bitten by a mosquito and died of an infection in Cairo on 5 April 1923, newspaper reports prompted the belief that he had been killed by a curse of the tomb. Other deaths or strange events connected with the tomb also came to be attributed to the curse.

An interesting article dealing with Egyptian curses appeared in the *Perth Sunday Times* for 6 May 1923:

The Priests' Curse – Strange Examples from the Past – Mummy Case Removed from Museum' 'Does black magic still exist? Many believe so. The death of Lord Carnarvon, attributed to the malign influence of ancient Egyptian priests, had caused a stir, and then came the news of the sudden illness of Mr Howard Carter, the deceased lord's right-hand man.

Millions refuse to attach more than coincidence to Lord Carnarvon's death, but it is a fact that a queer succession of tragedies forced the British Museum authorities to withdraw a notorious mummy case from exhibition. It has been alleged that the case was on board the ill-fated Titanic when she sank.

Thousands of years have rolled by, but still the secret of death and the hereafter is shrouded in mystery. In ancient times when the Pharaohs of Egypt reigned, the resting place of the dead was a spot sanctified by human memory, more so than in modern times. Today the hardened curse-proof sceptics look back cynically upon the invocations and malign influences that were supposed to be uttered. But the ancient Egyptians like many other advanced races, attached great religious significance to their dead. Many and curse-laden were the warnings they issued to the would-be exhumer and despoiler, and at odd intervals in the history of the twentieth century archaeological research there occur queer and seemingly unaccountable incidents.

There has been a sanctity attached to the dead through all the ages. Shakespeare expressed it briefly in 'Cursed be he that moves my bones.' Today, however, the grave excavator has a worthy cause to work for, that of scientific research, and what in the long ago would have been regarded as a mortal offence punishable by death is now encouraged.

Is there danger in this desecration of hundreds of years old tombs? Does the malign influence of the dead Pharaohs still exist? Those are the questions that have been exercising the minds of the greatest researchers. One of these long fingers of coincidence came to light in the finding of the ancient tomb of Tutankhamen at Luxor by Lord Carnarvon. Before he could look upon the mummy of the departed king Death laid its touch upon him, and now he has gone to seek what is hidden beyond. That fact and the knowledge that a malign influence was supposed to exist was enough to cause a sensation.

31

Sir Arthur Conan Doyle, the world-known spiritualist, gives his opinion that 'Powerful elementals or spirits placed on guard by the ancient Egyptian priests to protect the tomb may have caused the death of Lord Carnarvon. I consider it probable that during the Tutankhamen era the priests possessed the power to create guardian elements.'

Another well-known French spiritualist, M Lancelin, says: 'We do not know the extent of the powers of the ancient magicians, but it is certain that curses were uttered against the desecration of Tutankhamen's tomb.'

In London almost a panic was caused when this was made known. An avalanche of parcels containing mummies, shrivelled hands and feet, porcelain and wooden statues, and relics of ancient tombs descended on the British Museum. Some of them were valuable, while others were not of much account.

Lord Carnarvon's death just when he had arrived at the most important point is decidedly coincidental. That is taking into consideration the fact that similar happenings have been known. The potency of a specific curse uttered four or five thousand years ago is a debatable subject.

For those superstitious, the famous case of Tcheser-Ka-Ra, the High Priestess of Amen Ra, showed that the fulfilment of a desecration curse was swift and violent. The mummy itself was missing, so that the inscribed mummy case was alone responsible. This mummy case was placed in the British Museum, having already left a grim trail of accident and death in its wake.

Of the five archaeologists who had originally unearthed the coffin, one lost an arm, two lost their fortunes, and the fourth man died unaccountably. The fifth man, who conveyed the body to England, encountered misfortune after misfortune.

Later a photograph was taken of this unlucky mummy case, and, queerly enough, the face which appealed on the negative was diabolical in expression – a violent contrast to the contented and peaceful expression of the actual face on the lid of the case. A second attempt to photograph the face also failed, and shortly afterwards the photographer died.

The sinister reputation of the mummy case induced another photographer named George Davies to defy the inscribed curse and make a further attempt. From the moment he first handled the mummy case his sight commenced to fail, until eventually he was forced to undergo several operations. According to his stated opinion he was saved from total blindness only by destroying every photograph of the mummy case in his possession.

Forced by public opinion, the authorities of the Museum promptly withdrew the mummy case from exhibition. It has been alleged that this notorious mummy case was on board the ill-fated Titanic when she sank.

There are few nowadays who would think seriously that black magic still existed, but unaccountable examples such as these cause people to wonder. The fingers of coincidence are long, and many a cursed man has died inexplicably at the appointed hour.

How does the church view these things? Recently a 'Mail' man questioned Canon Wise, of Goodwood, upon that point.

'You have asked me,' said Canon Wise, 'if the Church has any views upon the matter of the lamented death of Lord Carnarvon, ascribed as it has been by certain people to the influence of priests of days gone by who still guard the sepulchres of the dead or who have laid a spell upon them, so that anyone who desecrates these sepulchres shall suffer hurt.

'The church has her own beliefs concerning her departed people, and she has nothing, so far as I know, in those beliefs that offer any support to the views of those stated above. The church believes in the sacredness of the human body as being the God-given tabernacle of the immortal soul and she regards any desecration of the dead as a most heinous offence. She bases her belief, of course, upon the fact of the resurrection of the body, and has, so far as I can see, always believed that holy angels guard the resting places of the bodies of her departed people.

'By reason of her influence it is that the laws are so severe upon any desecration of the dead. When it is necessary that a body shall be used in the interests of science, the parts of the body are always, so far as I know, carefully collected and reverently buried, and it is regarded as a hateful crime when any "body snatching" and so forth has been perpetrated. I believe that I am right in saying that the mind of the church rather revolts at first sight against this spoiling of the tombs of thousands of years ago, but most of us on further consideration would modify our views considerably and be fascinated by the great additions to knowledge that are likely to accrue from the spoiling.

'In the present case it has not been done from any sense of personal interest, but as a contribution, and apparently a most important one, to our knowledge of the past, and, while personally I consider it to be a crime against sentiment and to serve no useful end to take human bodies, however old, and place them in glass cases in museums, there seems to have been no such intention in the case of this present body, which would perhaps have been again buried and the tomb sealed, though the treasures themselves would be removed.

'At least we may, I am confident, assert from what we know of the late Lord Carnarvon and those associated with him that everything that was done has been done with all the reverence that learned men ever show in these cases.'

'We are living in days,' continued Canon Wise, 'when so many having neglected the old truths of religion and aware now of something missing in their lives are feverishly endeavouring to supply their loss. Hence, all modern superstitions are mostly reproductions of ancient heresies. This church in reality, though I know there are glaring exceptions in the past, has always been perfectly clear upon the sacredness of the dead, and while she reverently cares for their bodies she ever prays for their souls. The church has been equally clear upon the good influence of the departed upon those on earth, and she has relied upon the influence she believes they can and do exercise.

'If the dead priests of Egypt have the power to exercise malign influence upon those now living, their power should not be so great as that of the departed monarch himself. We cannot believe that one so great as he apparently is, and was, would now despite fully use one of his brethren, a philosopher and a savant like himself, who spent his talents and his wealth in striving to add to the store of human knowledge, and who was from all accounts, as are most great men, whatever their actual beliefs, a reverent soul and a believer in the good God.'

***

The story does not end there. London newspapers for 19 June 1927 carried the following strange story concerning what was seemingly the 'actual' mummy of Amen-Ra, under the title 'The Mummy of Amen-Ra – Mystery Crow Appears':

A month ago, Father Ward, director of the Abbey Folk Museum, New Barnet, bought at auction in London the mummy of Amen-Ra, high priest of Thebes, Egypt, who died in 580BC. A week after the mummy had been placed in the museum a big black crow appeared at the window of the building, and tapped on the pane. The bird has continued to appear since.

'I am inclined to think it is not a coincidence,' said Father Ward. 'The arrival of the bird may have something to do with the mummy; we never saw it before. Some might think there is something in the theory that the soul of a man returns in the form of a bird.'

Father John Sebastian Marlowe Ward (1885–1949) was a psychic medium and spiritualist. After the First World War he accumulated a significant private collection of antiques, and when from 1927 onwards he began to form the 'Confraternity of the Kingdom of Christ', together with his second wife Jessie, he would frequently return from a day in London to Park Road in New Barnet with their car laden with numerous historical pieces for the collection. It was opened as a church in 1930, and filled with genuine antiques.

The Folk Park Museum was one of the first of its kind in the world. Much of the collection was sold in 1945, but the rest still survives under the custodianship of the present members of his community at the Abbey Museum of Art and Technology in Caboolture, Queensland, Australia.

At the time of the sinking it was rumoured that the most famous – and most notorious gem – the Hope Diamond – was on board *Titanic* being secretly transported back to the United States in the charge of a courier on behalf of its owners, the newspaper magnate Edward Beale McLean (1889–1941), and his wife Evalyn (1886–1947), who had bought it from Pierre Cartier jewellers in New York in 1911.

Like the Amen-Ra coffin lid, throughout its history anyone who came into contact with it suffered misfortune. In 1919, their first child, Vinson, was hit by a car right in front of their house and died of his injuries aged only 9; their daughter died from an overdose of sleeping pills, and Ned McLean was eventually declared insane. Despite the jewel's reputation, Evalyn did not part with it until 1947. Newspapers reported on the sale:

> The Hope Diamond which has been sold for £60,000 is the finest of the four 'blue' diamonds known to collectors. It has been described as unique in colour, texture, and size.
>
> It measures 1½ inch by 7-8 inch. Its history is more or less a matter of speculation, but the generally received theory is that it is part of the Blue Diamond of the French Regalia which was put away in the Garde-Meubles in 1792. That stone disappeared; but many years afterwards David Eliason, a dealer, came into possession of what is believed to have been the French diamond, or part of it, in a re-cut form.
>
> It was this diamond that was bought by Thomas Hope, and that became known as the Hope Diamond. It is considerably smaller than the original French stone, but the experts believe that the chief remaining portion of the original is to be identified in another well-known stone, which was sold at Geneva at the sale of the Duke of Brunswick's jewels in 1874, and which is known as the Brunswick Blue Drop.

The *Australasia* newspaper of Melbourne carried an article on 14 August 1909 concerning the curse that seemed to be associated with the Hope Diamond. Although much of it is speculation, it makes for interesting reading:

> As a learned professor explained to the Anthropological Society a few years ago, magic rather than adornment was the original motive for wearing jewellery. Even I know the old superstition survives, and numbers of otherwise civilised people have a curious faith in the influences, good or evil, of certain gems, coins, and trinkets. Madame

Melba, for instance, shuns peacock's feathers, while Madame Esty is said never to sing in public without a small green heart, which she wears suspended from a light gold necklace. Many a cricket captain carries his luck-penny to toss with, and even Nelson had a horseshoe nailed to the mast of the Victory. Special stones frequently owe their occult reputation to the vicissitudes of their past owners. A notorious case in point is the famous blue Hope Diamond, which was sold in Paris [to Cartiers] a few weeks ago for the sum of £16,000. In view of its history, which has just been gravely related by 'The Times,' it is hardly surprising that the credulous should believe in its ill-luck.

It was first heard of in the latter half of the seventeenth century. A French traveller named Tavernier brought it back with him from the East, but ere long he was forced to sell his estate in order to pay his son's debts. The diamond was then bought by King Louis XIV as an addition to the Crown jewels of France. Madame de Montespan, in the heyday of her glory as Royal favourite, persuaded him to lend it to her. From about that time her influence over him began to wane, and in a little while she was supplanted in his affections by the 'widow Scarron' (Madame de Maintenon). Fouquet, the princely Superintendent of the Finances, next borrowed it for one of those gorgeous fetes in which he strove to outshine even his Royal master in magnificence. Soon afterwards he was disgraced and thrown into prison.

Then the diamond lay for years unheeded among the Crown jewels, until Louis XVI had it taken out for his ill-starred Queen, the beautiful Marie Antoinette: She is known to have worn it at one of the great balls at the Tuileries, and she also allowed her dear friend the Princess de Lamballe to wear it occasionally. Marie Antoinette died on the scaffold, and the Princess was done to death by the mob.

At the Revolution the gem was stolen, and its history for the ensuing 40 years is somewhat obscure. The story runs that Fals, an Amsterdam diamond cutter, was commissioned to cut it and that his son stole it from him. Fals was ultimately ruined, and his son committed suicide.

Young Fals is said to have given it to Francis Beaulieu, a native of Marseilles, who took it to London, and, a day before his death from starvation sold it to Eliason, the dealer. Anyhow, it is quite certain that Eliason sold it about 1830 for £18,000 to Henry Thomas Hope, son of the author of 'Anastasius'. It descended with the rest of the Hope Property to Lord Henry Francis Hope, who married May Yohe, the actress, and divorced her in 1902. In 1901 he obtained leave to sell the heirloom, whereupon it was purchased by Mr Weil, the London diamond merchant, who resold it at once to Frankel, a New York jeweller. Frankel could not find a purchaser, and got into financial straits.

Last year it passed into the hands of M Colot, a French broker, who disposed of it to the Russian Prince Kanitovski. The prince lent it to Lorens Ladue, a stage beauty of the Folies Bergere. The first night she wore it he shot her from the box in the theatre. Hating proved his right to the gem, he again took possession of it, but two days later he was himself stabbed by revolutionists. Thereupon Colot, the broker, went out of his mind and killed himself.

Of the diamond's further history *The Times* gives the following account: 'The next owner of the stone is stated to have been Simon Montharides, a Greek jeweller, who is said to have been thrown over a precipice and killed, with his wife and children. Montharides is stated to have sold the diamond to the ex-Sultan Abdul Hamid, whose passion for precious stones was well known. Whether the ex-Sultan ever owned the Hope Diamond is a point upon which it will perhaps be wise not to insist too strongly: but there is no possible doubt about the fact that it was in Constantinople until comparatively recently, and very little that it was in the Sultan's possession.

Its alleged adventures for the brief space while there seem to beggar the wildest fiction, and we give the story with all reserve. It is this. The Sultan gave it to Abu Sabir to be polished; he was bastinadoed [beating the soles of the feet with a stick], and thrown into a dungeon, from which he was rescued during the recent revolution. The keeper of the vault where the jewel was kept was found by the door strangled. Kulub Bey, the eunuch in whose charge it was placed, was one of those hanged in the streets by the Turkish mob.

Finally, and as if all these tragedies were insufficient to render the possession of the Hope Diamond a fearful joy, the Sultan's favourite, Salma Zubayba, was wearing it on her breast when the Young Turks broke into the Palace, and was shot dead by her master, the bullet striking close to the diamond.'

Even if the doubtful portions of its story be omitted the career of the Hope Diamond is yet full of romantic horrors.

Another newspaper of 9 July 1912, reported under the title 'The Titanic: Another Sea Mystery':

Superstitious people are seeing in the awful circumstances that the Titanic never finished her maiden voyage a predestined doom, and are connecting it with strange suggestions of ill-luck aboard.

The strangest of them all is based on a belief that the Hope Diamond was aboard the ill-fated ship and lived up to all the dread traditions of its name by casting the Titanic to the bottom of the sea.

It is a truly fantastic tale, but it will certainly find wide credence if by any chance the fact be ultimately established that the Hope diamond was really aboard. For a belief in good and ill-luck is universal, and the sanest and most matter-of-fact men own little superstitions which they would scarcely acknowledge even to themselves.

Ingrained in all human nature, however, is a very large element of superstition, and there are many travellers who would instantly feel misgivings if they learned that a jewel with so dire a history was aboard the Ship on which they were voyaging.

The Hope Diamond now belongs to a wealthy American lady, Mrs Evalyn McLean, who is a leading figure in Washington society. Some weeks ago, as the 'Daily Sketch' recorded at the time, the diamond was worn by its fair possessor at a reception given by Mrs McLean in honour of the new Russian Ambassador to the United States.

Stories were recalled of the tragic happenings which have followed the famous diamond everywhere, for it is reputed to be an unlucky stone – the unluckiest in the world. From the days when it shone on the fair neck of Queen Marie Antoinette and brought its wearer to the horrors of the French Revolution, every owner of its maleficent beauty is said to have been dogged by ill-fortune.

Mrs McLean wore the jewel in defiance of the Fates, wore it, too, in a costly setting composed of a magnificent circlet of pearls. Now, every woman knows that even pearls are linked with a tradition of ears. Many women are so superstitious on this point as to refuse to wear engagement or dress rings containing pearls, and shudder as such over pearls as others do at a gift of opals. Anyway, the setting was sufficient to emphasise rather than weaken the legend of the unlucky diamond, and rather than challenge the evil potentialities of the jewel a second time, so the story goes, Mrs McLean resolved to have her historic diamond reset. For this purpose 'The Hope' was recently sent to Amsterdam for expert handling.

Rumour says that the Hope Diamond was being secretly taken back to America in the care of a passenger on the Titanic. Inquiries have so far failed to confirm this, and for the present it is a mystery whether the unlucky jewel was or was not really among the many costly gems which were certainly being carried by the Titanic.

If it be true that the Hope diamond has sunk with the liner, its disappearance will be intrinsically an irreparable loss from a lady's jewel casket. But a world that has no room for anything that brings ill-fortune will heave something of a sigh of thankfulness to know that a sparkling lump of ill-luck has gone to the bottom of the sea.

However, the diamond was not among the jewellery recovered from *Titanic*, and it is now housed at the Smithsonian Institution.

4. SPIRITUAL WARNINGS

Lord William Pirrie, chairman of Harland and Wolff, was persuaded by his wife, Margaret, to go and have his fortune told by the celebrated Bond Street palmist Cheiro, who was making a big name for himself because of the many accurate prophesies he was giving. He included the Prince of Wales (later King Edward VII) among his clients, and would later foretell the death of Queen Victoria, the circumstances of the death of Lord Kitchener and the abdication of King Edward VIII. Margaret knew her husband had no interest in such things, so what may have prompted her to ask him to do it? Did she have feelings of foreboding?

The sitting took place in Bond Street in August 1899. The seer first mentioned that William had the hands of a child, and that he began his life far from home. William was born in Quebec, of Irish parentage, so Cheiro would have detected he did not have a truly English accent. He added that he saw a long voyage in William's past.

'And tomorrow?' William quizzed.

'You are about to be honoured in some way,' Cheiro replied.

After a short silence the palmist added quietly, 'And you will soon find yourself in a fight for your life.'

About a month later Lord William wrote to Cheiro stating that the Royal University of Ireland in Dublin was going to present him with an honorary law degree in recognition of his achievements in shipbuilding, and invited him to a tour of the shipyard if he was ever in Belfast.

The meaning of the reference to a 'fight for your life' is not clear. He had heard that a rival businessman named J Pierpoint Morgan was attempting to take control of the North Atlantic shipping industry, which was *soon*, but that was hardly a fight for *his* life, more the fight *of* his life.

William Pirrie was born in Quebec on 24 May 1847, the son of James Alexander Pirrie and Elizabeth Margaret Swan Montgomery, who were both Irish. His grandfather was Captain William Pirrie, a Belfast ship owner and harbour commissioner who encouraged his grandson's maritime ambitions. They returned to live in Ireland when William was aged two, at Colig in County Down. He attended the Royal Belfast Academicals Institute before entering Harland and Wolff as a premium apprentice in 1862. In 1874 he was made a partner and became chairman in 1895, a position he maintained until his death on 7 June 1924.

Several London newspapers for 8 June 1924, reported – 'Death of Lord Pirrie – Greatest Shipping Organiser':

> The death is announced by wireless of the Viscount Pirrie, the greatest shipping and shipbuilding organizer in the world, which occurred while he was on a voyage from Buenos Aires to New York – Reuter. Lord Pirrie, who was head of the firm of Harland & Wolff, Limited, shipbuilders, died suddenly on Saturday night, from bronchial pneumonia, on board the steamer Ebro, on which he was returning from a visit to South American ports to study shipping prospects. Viscountess Pirrie accompanied him on the voyage. The body will arrive at New York on Friday, and will be sent to Ireland on board the Cedric, which sails on Saturday. There is no heir to the title.

***

John Pierpoint Morgan (1837–1913) had intended to sail on *Titanic*'s maiden voyage but later decided to remain relaxing in the French resort of Aix. He was nicknamed 'The Napoleon of Wall Street' and he had helped to create the General Electric Company and US Steel, and he was credited with being foremost in saving the United States banking system during the panic of 1907. He had attended the launch of *Titanic* in 1911 and had a personal suite on board with his own promenade deck and a bath equipped with specially designed cigar holders. He died in his sleep in a hotel in Rome.

An associate of his was Henry Clay Frick (1849–1919), the Pittsburgh steel baron. Frick had also intended to travel on *Titanic* but was forced to cancel his passage after his wife sprained her ankle and had to be hospitalised in Rome.

***

The psychic investigator and spiritualist Archdeacon Thomas Colley had written to W T Stead forecasting the disaster and of possible

40

misfortune for him and his wife in their future. On 9 April 1912, Stead wrote back to him stating: 'Thank you very much for your kind letter, which reached me just as I am starting for America. I sincerely hope that none of the misfortunes which you seem to think might happen to myself or my wife will happen, but I will keep your letter, and write to you when I come back.'

His wife was his childhood sweetheart, Emma Lucy Wilson. She lived to the age of 82, and died on 22 February 1932.

Archdeacon Colley was an eccentric psychical investigator and rector of Stockton near Rugby from 1901 until his death in 1912 (who printed a pamphlet entitled *The Foreordained Wreck of the Titanic*. A report of his death appeared in the *Rugby Advertiser*:

> The Reverend Thomas Colley, commonly known as Archdeacon Colley, died at his lodgings in Middlesbrough at 10 o'clock on Monday night, after attending the Church Union there. He was appointed, in 1879, Archdeacon of Pietermaritzburg by Bishop Colenso, and he clung to the title of Archdeacon for the rest of his life. He was presented in 1901 to the living of Stockton, in the diocese of Worcester, but a freak ceremony which he conducted last January led to his resignation.
>
> Mr Colley caused his glass-topped coffin, which for eight years had been kept in the rectory, to be removed to the church, and after evensong he placed himself in his vestments, inside his coffin, and was borne from the chancel to the west door and back again, in full view of the congregation. He then rose, and, standing in the coffin, wished the parishioners 'A Happy New Year!' He explained that he wished to teach the truth that death is the gate of life, and rehearse the scene which would take place before his remains should someday be sent to Birmingham for dissection, he having bequeathed his body to the Dean of the Medical Faculty of Birmingham University for anatomical purposes. It seems (so says the 'Times') that Mr Colley further contemplated that, when dissection had been completed, his bones should be wired together and deposited in the psychic museum at Leamington.

***

W T Stead had also consulted Cheiro, who warned him against travelling on such a ship, especially in the month of April. He told Stead: 'I see more than a thousand people, you among them, struggling desperately in the water. They are screaming for help and fighting for their lives. But it does none of them any good . . . yourself included!'

The *Sydney Truth* published an article by Cheiro on 26 August 1951, titled 'He Flirted with 'Fate' – And Died At Sea', which gives an interesting aspect of this palm-reading session:

W T Stead, the celebrated author and editor of the *Review of Reviews*, knew the month and year of his death, because I told him.

We met in Paris, and as I was wearing the decoration which had been given me by the Shah of Persia because I had predicted the date of his attempted assassination. Mr Stead made me explain how I worked out my theory of numbers by what might be called 'Fadic' dates.

When I had finished explaining my reasons for picking out the date of the attempt on the Shah's life he asked me to tell him some things about the characters of people whose numbers, according to my system, were keys to their characters and the chief events of their lives.

When I had finished he told me that the numbers he had given me were those of his own sons, and as far as he could judge, the picture I had made was exact even to the smallest detail of character.

Mr Stead had the firm conviction that his death would be one of violence at the hands of a London mob.

I believe he had this idea from the time a mob attacked his offices and smashed the windows, apparently as an indication of the feeling engendered by his opposition to the Boer War.

Mr Stead on more than one occasion referred to this extraordinary belief of his. The last time he brought the matter up was in the middle of June 1911, when he had lunch with me at my house. I argued against his view, as I always did, but again I failed to make him change his mind.

My words, however, had made some impression on him, for a few days later he telephoned me and asked me to consider the matter again, letting him know the result.

The following is a copy of a letter I sent to him. It is dated 21 June 1911:

'Yes, I remember very clearly our discussion at lunch here the other day, but I see no reason to go back on what I said then, namely, that as far as I can judge, you need have no reason to believe that your life will end by violence from a London mob.

'I have gone over very carefully the impression of your hand that you gave me many years ago, also the more recent notes I made on it, and judging from it and from the date of your birth in the sign of Cancer, otherwise known as the First House of Water, in my humble opinion, any danger of violent death to you must be from water and nothing else. The most important months for you to avoid travelling in are December, and next April of 1912.

'Very critical and dangerous for you should be April, 1912, especially about the middle of that month. So don't travel by water then if you can help it. If you do you will be liable to meet with such danger to your life that the very worst may happen.

'I know I am not wrong with this "water" danger; I only hope I am, or at least that you will not be travelling somewhere about that period.'

The following month I went to Spain, and the rest is history. Nine months later, in April 1912, I was on board an Italian liner in the Mediterranean when the captain announced to the passengers that he had received a message that the Titanic had sunk, and among other names of those lost he read out that of W T Stead.

Stead told his friends and colleagues about the warning, and pointed out how it tied in with the fictitious articles he had published in 1886 and 1892.

***

Lifeboat 7 was the first to be lowered from *Titanic* at about 12.45am, and while it was being rowed away from the doomed ship and across the Atlantic waters, Helen Margaret Walton Bishop (1892–1916) made a comment that, although it was strange, probably gave some comfort to her fellow survivors through her optimism: 'We have to be rescued for the rest of my prophecy to come true.'

The reason for the remark was that while she and her new husband, a wealthy young American businessman named Dickinson H Bishop (1887–1961), who had been married previously, were honeymooning in Egypt she decided to visit a fortune teller. The seer divined her future, saying that she would survive a shipwreck, and an earthquake, before an automobile accident would end her life. Helen was pregnant at the time of the sinking, but she lost the baby, who they had named Randall Walton, only two days into his life – something the fortune teller appears to have failed to mention.

During another vacation in California an earthquake jolted the couple – which fulfilled the second part of the Egyptian's prophecy. On 15 November 1913, the couple were returning home from Kalamazoo in their car when it went out of control and struck a tree. Helen suffered a severely fractured skull and was not expected to live. However, she recovered, but had to have a steel plate placed in her skull. The mental and physical trauma caused a change in her personality; consequently, the Helen her husband had known seems to have died, the marriage suffered, and they were divorced in January 1916. Helen died on 16 March 1916, after suffering a bad fall.

***

Walter Harris (1867–1912) was having tea with friends just before leaving home in Walthamstow, when one of the party, who practised palmistry, looked at his hand and although she was reluctant to say what it had revealed, she remarked that she 'did not like it'. 'Is daddy going to be drowned?' asked Harris's little son, Walter Ernest.

Walter was on his way to the home of Charles Oxenham, and made the trip with Charles's younger brother, Percy Thomas Oxenham (1890–1954). Percy survived the disaster, but Walter lost his life, and if his body was recovered, it was not identified.

5. THE LAP OF THE GODS

There were many stories of people who should have travelled on *Titanic* but for various reasons they did not do so and had a lucky escape. Such strange forebodings can be found in many books prior to the *Titanic* disaster.

In his 1912 book *Campaigns of a War Correspondent*, Melton Prior, a well-known artist and correspondent with the *Illustrated London News*, stated:

I am now going to mention a subject of which I am not particularly proud. I had been through several campaigns, some of them very disagreeable ones. I had run my risks and fear had never entered my mind, but unfortunately, on my journey out on this occasion, I had a bad dream. I call it a dream, but I think it must have been a nightmare. It took place after I had arrived in Durban [to cover the Zulu War of 1879].

Now this nightmare had such an effect on me that I have never forgotten it. I dreamt that I went with the relieving force to rescue Colonel Pearson at Eshowe. I saw myself shot and I saw myself buried.

Strange to say, by the next mail arriving from England I received a letter from my mother, in which she told me she had had a dream that I had gone with the relieving column to Eshowe, that I had been killed, and that she had seen my funeral, and she wound up by begging me most earnestly not to go with that column, and it is now that I am ashamed to own up that this had such an effect on me that I made up my mind I would not go, and even wrote to Mr William Ingram at my office to inform him of my determination. Some weeks later I received a cablegram from him: 'Sorry you did not accompany the force, no doubt saved for better things to come.'

However, I did not wish the *Illustrated* to be unrepresented in the expedition, and I succeeded in enlisting the services of Colonel Crealock, the Chief of Staff, and also engaged the services of a private individual named Porter.

Now came the curious incident of this act of mine. When the fighting did take place at Ginghilovo, on the road to Eshowe, my specially appointed artist was one of the first killed.

Whether I believe in presentiment may or may not be interesting to anyone, but this case is surely curious.

***

A crew reorganisation saved the life of one of *Titanic*'s officers, while his replacement went down with the ship. The original ranking of the senior officers on *Titanic* were Chief Officer William McMaster Murdoch (1873–1912); First Officer Charles Herbert Lightoller (1874–1952); and Second Officer David Blair (1874–1955). Henry Tingle Wilde (1872–1912) had been expecting to remain as chief officer on RMS *Olympic*, under Captain Herbert James Haddock (1861–1946), but instead he was posted to Southampton to await orders. RMS *Olympic* had been laid up, so Captain Haddock had been placed in charge of *Titanic* while the Liner was in Belfast, until 1 April, when he took over as captain of *Olympic* and Edward Smith became captain of *Titanic*.

Olympic eventually sailed out of Southampton on 3 April with many of her officers and crew having been transferred to *Titanic*. These included Wilde, who transferred as chief officer on 9 April, and Blair was removed from *Titanic*'s roster. This meant the officers had to reorganise, and William Murdock became first officer, while Charles Lightoller became second officer.

In a letter to his sister posted when the ship reached Queenstown, the new Chief Officer Wilde lamented, 'I still don't like this ship . . . I have a queer feeling about it.' Henry Wilde lost his life in the sinking, and if his body was recovered, it was never identified. Part of the inscription dedicated to him on a grave in Kirkdale Cemetery, Liverpool, says he was 'One of Britain's Heroes'.

Seven weeks after the disaster, Captain Haddock narrowly avoided running *Olympic* on to rocks near Land's End, apparently through faulty navigation.

***

The *Southampton Times and Hampshire Express* for 20 April 1912 interviewed the mother of three local Southampton men named Slade, who should have been on the ship. They were Alfred Edward (aged 25), Bertram (aged 26) and Thomas (aged 27). Mrs Slade is recorded as saying: 'What a good job they missed their ship! I have thanked God ever since. How did they miss the boat? I can't tell you but they left home in good time.

'Somehow or other my boys did not seem very keen on going on the ship. You may not believe in dreams, but I am telling you the truth when I say that one of my boys had a dream about the boat the night before sailing day, and he afterwards said that he had a dread of her. I knew they were not very keen on going but nevertheless they went down.'

The hiring of the *Titanic* crew began on Friday, 6 April, and the experienced Slade brothers were all taken on as firemen. Bertram and Thomas had worked on RMS *Olympic*, which had berthed at Southampton on 30 March 1912, and youngest brother Alfred had been working on the *Highland Glen*.

The crew was ordered to board *Titanic* to muster at eight o'clock on the morning of 10 April, and be ready to sail at twelve o'clock noon. It would seem that the three brothers met up with other members of the crew at the Grapes Hotel for a last drink before boarding. They left the pub at about 11.50am to go back to the ship, but as they approached the dock gates, a train came out and blocked their way. Two members of the group dashed across the front of the train, but the Slade brothers decided to wait and let it pass. Unfortunately, this made them late, and as they hurried towards the last gangway to be lowered, which was on E-deck close to the stern, they were told that they were too late and had been replaced by other men. To add insult to injury they were reported as 'deserters'.

Lawrence Beesley later stated: 'Just before the last gangway was withdrawn a knot of stokers ran along the quay, with their kit slung over their shoulders and bundles, and made for the gangway, with the evident intention of joining the ship. But a petty officer guarding the shore end of the gangway firmly refused to allow them on board; they argued, gesticulated, apparently attempting to explain the reasons why they were late, but he remained obdurate and waved them back with a determined hand, and the gangway was dragged back amid their protests . . .'

***

John Coffey (1890–1957) joined *Titanic* at Southampton as a fireman. He was scheduled to complete the journey to New York and back, but he chose to depart the liner when it docked at Queenstown after he said he had experienced a strange foreboding about the voyage.

It has been suggested that he may have only taken on the job so he could get a free ride to Queenstown, which was his home town, and always intended to leave the ship. He later joined RMS *Mauritania*, and eventually settled at Kingston upon Hull, where a newspaper of 1940 reported that he had to be rescued after falling into the river.

***

Harry Burrows lived with his mother at 38 Anderson's Road, Southampton, and made his living working on board the great liners that sailed from that port city. Burrows had been anticipating getting a berth on the new *Titanic*, so much so that he had stayed home for a month so that he would be available when the time came.

On 10 April Burrows bade his mother goodbye and went down to the dock to sign on the great liner. A little while later, however, Mrs Burrows was surprised to see her son returning to the house. He had not signed on *Titanic* after all.

Mrs Burrows later spoke to the press about this incident concerning her son. Harry Burrows, she said, had 'at the last minute changed his mind and come away, for which we are very grateful. I can't explain why he changed his mind; some sort of feeling came over him, he told me.'

***

Twenty-four-year-old Alex Mackenzie had travelled down from Glasgow and was walking up the gangway to board *Titanic* when a voice suddenly warned him that if he got on the ship he would never get off. He looked all around but there was no one else present. He shook off the warning and walked on, only to hear the warning a second time, and then a third, with each warning sounding stronger than the one previous. It was then that he decided to abandon his trip and return to Glasgow. His parents were understandably displeased at first for him having wasted an expensive ticket – until a few days later when news of the *Titanic* disaster reached them.

***

John Connan Middleton (1865–1917) was a British banker, who was vice-president of the Akron-Canton Railway of Ohio and had served as British vice-consul at Monterey in Mexico from 1893 to 1897.

On 17 April 1912, the Honourable John Connan Middleton wrote a letter from his home at Winchester House in London to the editor of the *Journal of the Society for Psychical Research,* in which he referred to premonitory dreams he had:

It may be of interest to you to learn that on 23 March I booked my passage to New York on the White Star liner 'TITANIC'. About ten days before she sailed I dreamt that I saw her floating on the sea, keel upwards, and her passengers and crew swimming round her.

Although I am not given to dreaming at all, I was rather impressed with this dream, but I disclosed it to no one, as my friends beside my wife and family knew that I was about to sail on 'Titanic' and I did not want to cause them any uneasiness.

The following night, however, I had the very same dream, and I must admit that then I was somewhat uncomfortable about it. Still, I said nothing to anyone and had all my trunks packed, business affairs arranged, had given up my room at the hotel, and in fact had completed all my plans to sail on the 10th instant. I merely awaited the receipt of a cable from some business friends about certain matters that would require my presence in America. The cable came a few days before the date of sailing (4 April to be exact), but it suggested that I should postpone my sailing for a few days. I thereupon cancelled my ticket, and then, that is, more than a week before the sailing of the 'Titanic' – I told my wife and several friends of the vivid dreams I had had on two consecutive nights.

I may mention that, previous to cancelling my passage, I felt most depressed and even despondent, but ascribed this feeling to the fact of my having to leave England – home sickness, in fact! Parenthetically, I may mention that my brother, whom I had not seen for twenty-five years, was to arrive from the East on the evening of the 10th, and I would thus have missed seeing by a few hours, and, as things have turned out, never [seen] him again.

Beyond a few passing remarks very little was said or thought about my dreams, and you may imagine the state of my mind (not to mention my deep gratitude for my personal escape), and that of my friends when the wireless message of the disaster flashed to this country. Among the friends to whom I told my dreams days before the 10th was the inventor of submarine signalling.

I have my ticket, cables, etc, in support of what I have written, but I do not know whether what I have said is of any interest to your Society, but if it is, I shall be glad to send you any copies you may wish or show you the originals.

I may add that crossing the Atlantic is nothing new to me, as I have crossed it a dozen times during the last few years, and I never remember having any feeling of uneasiness when about to do so or during the passage.

On 15 April William James Feddon sent a letter of corroboration to the society:

I, William James Feddon, merchant in the city of London, EC, hereby declare that a fortnight ago a friend of mine who was to be a passenger on board the SS Titanic, advertised to sail from Southampton on the 10th April, said to me that he was glad that his intended voyage thereon was not to take place for the reason that he had on two occasions dreamt that the ship was being wrecked. The cause of his not going was owing to the fact that he had received cable instructions to postpone his sailing, and as a consequence the ticket taken for the Titanic was cancelled.

Mr Middleton sent the society a letter he had received from Lucien I Blake, consulting engineer, Submarine Signal Company, dated 25 April:

Dear Mr Middleton; In reply to your letter of the 19th inst, I beg to say that I recall that, about ten days previous to the Titanic disaster, you told me at breakfast that you had had a dream for two consecutive nights of seeing a large vessel bottom up and people swimming about it. I remember remarking to you that, according to tradition, if you had the same dream for three nights, the incident must come to pass. This is all I recall.

The society received another letter from Jesse H Curling, dated 23 April:

Mr Middleton told me about April 5th or 6th, on more than one occasion, that he had had a most curious dream about the Titanic being wrecked and going down in mid-ocean. He said he saw most distinctly the ship sinking and on her side, and all the people in the water struggling. He said it was an awful sight, and quite unnerved him. I asked him several questions about it at the time, as I was rather impressed by the way it had got on his nerves, as he is a strong-minded man, and especially as I did not believe in dreams myself. I asked him where he was; and he said he seemed to be floating in the air above the wreck, and said he could see all the people in the water, all around. He said he had cancelled his ticket. I thought a great deal of what he had told me, and I told others about it at the time.

The *Journal* stated:

On 2 May 1912 Mr Middleton came to 20 Hanover Square [headquarters of the Society] and saw Miss Newton. Miss Newton's report of the meeting is as follows: 'Mrs Middleton said that her husband told her that on two consecutive nights he had dreamed of a ship "turned turtle" and numbers of people struggling in the water, he himself floating above but not in the water. She asked him not to sail in the Titanic, but he laughed and said how foolish it would seem if he postponed his business on account of a dream. He telephoned during the morning that he had received a cable to delay his departure, and that consequently he had cancelled his berth on the Titanic. Mrs Middleton describes him as a sensible business man, who has never attached importance to dreams, premonitions, impressions, etc. She said, 'He never dreams,' and, most emphatically, that he had never had a dream of this kind before.

In a letter written on 1 May 1912, Mr Middleton, relating to the date at which he related his dream, says:

I did not tell my wife about [the dream] until I had cancelled my ticket, which was on the 4th, as I felt sure that had I done so it would have caused her a great deal of worry, and in fact it was not my intention to tell her anything about it at all, had I not received the cable which altered my plans. I am positive of the fact that on April 4th I told my wife, because that was the day on which I received the cable. I had previously told my friends, Feddon, Curling and Blake, and while I cannot recall the exact date of this, I think it was about four or five days before I had received the cable from America.

The society responded:

It will be seen that there is some discrepancy in these statements as to the exact date at which Mr Middleton related his dream. In his original letter of 17 April 1912, he says that he told no one of his dream until after he had received the cable (4 April), but on May 1 he writes that he had told three friends of it before that date. The statements from Mr Feddon and Mr Curling imply that Mr Middleton had cancelled his passage at the time when he spoke to them of his dream, and therefore corroborate Mr Middleton's original statement; Mr Blake's statement leaves this question open.

There is also a discrepancy between the statements of Mr and Mrs Middleton. Both agree that April 4 was the day on which Mrs Middleton heard of the dream, but whereas Mr Middleton maintains throughout that he did not mention the matter to his wife until he had decided to cancel his passage, Mrs Middleton says that she heard of the dream on the morning of April 4 before the cable had been received. All the witnesses, however, are agreed that they heard of the dream sometime before the wreck of the Titanic, which it will be remembered, happened

51

on the night of April 14–15 1912, and the above discrepancies are only worth pointing out as an instance of the difficulty of getting exact testimony in a matter of this sort, even in regard to quite recent events.

Mr Middleton has also submitted to us the cable which caused him to delay his departure, marked with the date of receipt, 9.40am, April 4 1912, and his ticket for the Titanic.

***

On 4 July 1912, an associate of the Society for Psychical Research named Alice L Head of Bayswater sent a letter concerning someone who lived in her household. Alice stated that she had seen the letters, signed by Margaret Simpson, but to respect the wishes of those involved, the society used pseudonyms.

The lady in question was Miss Margaret Simpson, who lost a brother on *Titanic*. The brother had served on other vessels of the White Star Line, but he had been compelled to resign because of illness. However, just before *Titanic* sailed he was offered and accepted a post on the ship. This was known to Margaret, but not to a married sister, who had become Mrs Henderson, of Vancouver.

On 19 April 1912, Mrs Henderson wrote to Margaret's sister in Clifton, Bristol, Miss Emma Simpson, stating, 'I was busy in the afternoon after lunch, on Tuesday April 16, and I saw Bessie and Nina crying and clinging to one another. I seemed to be in a kind of dream and yet I was wide awake and had not even been thinking of them.'

Bessie and Nina were the wife and child of Mr Simpson.

In reply to questions from Margaret, Mrs Henderson wrote again on 13 June, 'You asked me about seeing Bessie and Nina; I was alone in the house, and they seemed to appear to me in a kind of mist; I could not see their faces. Had I been thinking of them at the time, I could understand it, but I was busy after lunch.

'I did not know anything about Willie's illness then, or that he was on the Titanic, but I had no doubt that it was Bessie and Nina that I saw. I told Cissy and Daisy about it that evening (16 April 1912).'

Although the society published the letter in the journal, because of the use of pseudonyms they gave no opinion concerning the information.

***

Lieutenant Commander Norman Carlyle Craig had a providential escape. Born in 1868, he was the Conservative Member of Parliament for the Isle of Thanet from 1910 until his death in 1919.

In 1912, he booked a passage to America on board RMS *Titanic*. However, he cancelled his trip at such short notice that his name still appeared on the printed list of *Titanic*'s first-class passengers. This led to early newspaper reports that he was among the victims of the sinking. He actually died on 14 October 1919 after failing to recover from an unspecified operation.

An American passenger named Charles Moore had planned to transport as many as a hundred English foxhounds on *Titanic*, with the intention of starting an English-style fox hunt, but he made arrangements for them to travel on a different vessel at the last minute.

One person who breathed a sigh of relief was a Mr L Wells, who received a message telling of the sinking of *Titanic* while he was on his way from England to Australia aboard SS *Orsova* soon after the disaster. His sister and her husband had been booked to sail on the doomed ship, but they changed their mind at the last minute.

Another person who shared Mr Middleton's good luck was Colin Macdonald, a 34-year-old marine engineer, who was offered the post of second engineer on *Titanic*. He turned the job down three times, and in 1964 his daughter told a leading American psychical researcher that her late father had experienced a 'strong impression that something awful was going to happen to the Titanic'. The man who eventually took the job as second engineer on *Titanic* was drowned.

***

Guglielmo Marconi (1874–1937), the man who had invented the wireless equipment that was used on *Titanic*, had been offered a free passage on the ship, but he decided to travel on *Lusitania* three days earlier because, as his daughter, Degna, later explained, he had paperwork to do and preferred the public stenographer aboard the latter vessel. He was booked on *Titanic* for the return trip that never happened.

***

The London Symphony Orchestra had planned to sail on *Titanic* on their way to a three-week tour of the United States and Canada. However, the tour was rescheduled to begin at an earlier date and they travelled on board SS *Baltic* during the previous week. On 2 July 1912, they took part in a 'Great Memorial Concert' for the benefit of the *Titanic* band:

Under the auspices of the Orchestral Association of England a great memorial concert was given in the Royal Albert Hall, London, on Friday,

May 24 last (Empire Day) in honour of the Titanic bandsmen who perished on the Titanic on April l5 last. A copy of the programme has been received from London by Mr James Booth.

The orchestra was composed of 100 instrumentalists, chosen from seven of the leading orchestras of London. The conductors were Sir Edward Elgar (London Symphony Orchestra), Sir Henry J Wood (Queen's Hall Orchestra), Mr Landon Ronald (Now Symphony Orchestra), Mr Thomas Beecham (Beecham Symphony Orchestra), Mr Percy Pitt (Musical Director of the Royal Opera House), M Fritz Ernanldy (London Opera House), and Herr Mengelberg, each of whom led the musicians in chosen numbers. Among the compositions played were Chopin's 'Funeral March' and 'Nearer, My God, to Thee.' Madame Ada Crossley, the famous Australian singer, also contributed to the programme.

***

Thomas Hart was aged 49 when he signed on *Titanic* as a fireman. He had been born in Manchester, and was living at 51 College Road in Southampton when he reported for duty on 6 April 1912. However, he went to the local hostelry to celebrate his new job on the night before boarding, where he drank heavily, apparently dozed off, and when he woke up, his discharge book was gone. Following the theft he walked about Southampton in a confused state, too ashamed and disappointed in himself to return home.

A man reported for duty on the following morning who produced a 'certificate of continuous discharge' bearing the name of Thomas Hart in gold leaf. He would have been on duty in one of the engine rooms when the ship collided with the iceberg. The job of the firemen was to feed the furnaces with coal brought to them by 'trimmers'. There were twenty-nine boilers, which powered the three massive engines. The men who worked in this department were known as the 'Black Gang' because of their dirty appearance, and they were rarely seen by the passengers.

It was never determined who stole Tom's credentials, but whoever it was, it was a case of rough justice as he lost his life in the disaster, and if his body was found, it was never identified.

Tom's family were notified by the White Star Line that he had lost his life in the tragedy, and his grieving mother began to make arrangements for her supposedly drowned son's memorial service, and employed a firm of Liverpool solicitors to act on behalf of the family. It is hard to imagine the mixed emotions of shock and joy she must have felt on 8 May when Tom walked into their home alive and well, if somewhat embarrassed.

In James Cameron's film an infamous game of cards (or chance) took place in which Leonardo DiCaprio gambled with his ship's papers. This scene is based on the Thomas Hart incident.

***

A strange event happened in early 1928 when Mrs E Robertson telephoned the local newspaper at Coalville in Leicestershire enquiring if her mother was still alive. She had left home to board *Titanic* but had cancelled her booked passage on the ill-fated liner at the last minute. She told nobody of her intentions and therefore they thought she had gone down with the ship. Her shocked mother *was* alive and one of her sisters met her at the train station. She stated that she had been doing war work and that she had been captured by the Germans.

On 13 February 1928, under the title 'Titanic Victim Returns', the *Queensland Daily Mercury* reported the following strange event:

> One of the supposed victims among the 1500 odd who were drowned when the Titanic sank in the North Atlantic in April 1912, after striking an iceberg on her maiden voyage to America, has reappeared after nearly 16 years' silence. This is Mrs E Robertson, who has visited her home at Coalville, Leicestershire (says the 'Calcutta Statesman').
>
> Her explanation is that she cancelled her booked passage to America on the ill-fated vessel at the last moment. She says she has done war work, and that she was captured by the Germans, but she gave no details of her later movements. Mrs Robertson visited Coalville to see her mother, whose shock on seeing her was only mitigated by the fact that her daughter had telephoned to a local paper inquiring if her mother was still alive. Another daughter met her at the train station. Mrs Robertson stayed at Coalville for two nights, and then left without giving any indication of her future movements.

55

6. BAD FOREBODINGS (CREW)

It is known that sailors and the crews of ships are superstitious and sometimes harbour bad forebodings about their coming voyages, and frequently the bad feelings proved to be true. For instance, a sailor named William Marshfield of the Royal Navy left an account about one particular let-off he had:

> I am a superstitious man, a man with what are called presentiments. Everybody knows what presentiments are, but no one has ever been able to explain them. You are overwhelmed with a sense of coming evil – that is what presentiment means.
>
> In the early part of 1870 I was drafted to HMS *Captain*. From the moment that order was given I was so filled with a foreboding of disaster that I went to the length of vowing that rather than go to sea in the ship I would leave the service. It was no good reasoning with or laughing at me; it was useless to say that the *Captain* was designed by a famous man, and that he himself had so much faith in the vessel that he was going to sea in her. I refused to be laughed or talked out of my forgiving, and at last, by a stroke of luck, I got transferred to HMS *Excellent*, gunnery ship.
>
> The *Captain* sailed a few months afterwards, and during the night capsized in the Bay of Biscay, carrying with her nearly all her officers and men, as well as her confiding designer. Only the watch on deck, less than a score of souls, was saved.

It would seem that Seaman Marshfield was somewhat unlucky, as he was boatswain on HMS *Calliope* when it had to be rescued during a hurricane off Samoa in 1889; and again during the loss of HMS *Victoria* when it was rammed and sunk in the Mediterranean Sea in 1893.

***

Some members of the crew who had sailed on *Olympic* had expressed foreboding about that ship, and these apprehensive feelings did not fade when they transferred to *Titanic*. *Olympic* suffered several mishaps during her first months afloat. The most serious of these was during her fifth voyage on 20 September 1911, with Captain Edward Smith in charge. She was cruising in the Solent off the Isle of Wight when HMS *Hawke* came parallel to her and they eventually collided so severely that *Hawke* lost her bow in the incident, and *Olympic* had her hull badly damaged. During an inquiry it was decided that the vast amount of water displaced by the large liner had generated a suction that had drawn *Hawke* off course, and *Olympic* was blamed. The White Star Line lodged an appeal but lost the decision.

In two further accidents she struck a sunken wreck and had to have a broken propeller replaced, and she nearly ran aground on one occasion while she was leaving Belfast. To get her back to service quickly after the damage, Harland and Wolff had to pull resources from *Titanic*, which fatefully delayed her maiden voyage by three weeks, from 20 March to 10 April.

***

A seaman named Arthur John 'Jack' Priest (1887–1937), a native of Southampton, was on the liner at the time, and he survived so many shipping accidents, including the *Titanic* disaster, that he was nicknamed 'The Unsinkable'. The *Times* for 23 April 1917 carried the following report:

> The remarkable adventures of a young fireman have been brought to light through the sinking of the *Donegal*.
>
> Arthur John 'Jack' Priest, who lives in Southampton, is only 29 years of age. He has now been on the sea since his youth, and has served on many waters. He has seen four of the vessels in which he was serving sink, and three others have been damaged. Several years ago [1908] he was in the 'Asturias' when she met with an accident on her maiden voyage. He was one of the survivors of the disaster which overtook the 'Titanic' on her maiden voyage five years ago, escaping with frost-bitten toes and an injured leg.
>
> He was also in the 'Olympic' when that vessel and the 'Hawke' came into collision near the Isle of Wight some years ago, and he served in the 'Alcantra' during her gallant fight with the German raider 'Greif' in the North Sea.
>
> The 'Alcantra' was sunk by a torpedo and Priest was wounded by shrapnel during the fight. Later he joined the 'Britannic', and was

serving in that ship when she sank last November. His last ship was the 'Donegal' from which he escaped with a rather serious injury to his head.

***

Only a few weeks after the disaster, newspapers had already noticed the unusual number of out of the ordinary events that had occurred in connection with *Titanic,* and the *Daily Mail* reported on some of the many premonitions, which their correspondent put down to vivid imaginations:

How strangely imagination may anticipate history has seldom been more remarkably shown than in the disaster to the Titanic.

About two months ago a number of officers of the White Star liners, Olympic and Irishman, were with their wives having tea at Southampton when conversation turned on superstitions and prophecies. It was jokingly mentioned that a prophecy had been published by one of the seers that about this time of the year the largest vessel in the world would sink. A number of the Olympic's officers, including the captain, were to be transferred to the Titanic, and there was humorous speculation aboard as to whether the ban rested on the Olympic or the Titanic. Captain Smith said: 'Well, if the largest liner in the world goes down, I shall go down with her.'

An extraordinary story of a passenger's presentiment of coming disaster to the Titanic is related by a well-known solicitor. Barely a day before the Titanic sailed, he said, 'A wealthy businessman came to me, and considerably surprised me by asking if I could consent to be a guardian to his two little boys. I naturally asked him what he meant, and he replied: "Tomorrow I and my wife are sailing on the Titanic. I cannot tell you why, but I feel that something is going to happen, and that we shall never see our children again." 'Up to the present,' continued the solicitor, 'neither his name nor that of his wife appear among the saved.'

Two other apparently well-authenticated cases of premonition of the disaster are related. One man who sailed from Southampton, said to be a fireman named Coffey, having grave, indefinable misgivings, left the boat at Queenstown. Another, a steward, is stated to have told his wife before his departure that he wished he had not signed on.

A press representative, who inspected the Titanic prior to her departure from Southampton, communicates the following incident which occurred at the official luncheon on board. The tables were laid in the centre of one of the rooms, and just previous to the few short speeches that were delivered one of the tables collapsed. This was much commented upon, the hope being expressed that no mishap would happen to the mammoth liner after she left port.

Reference to Old Moore and Zadkiel's Almanacs recall to mind the fact that the eclipse, the greatest this country has seen for fifty-three years, followed within a few hours of the Titanic disaster. The former sage writes for mid-April shipping: 'Shipping affairs will be disordered. This country is threatened with disaster.' Zadkiel writes: 'There will be depression in New York.'

Six firemen who had been signed on reached the quayside at Southampton last Wednesday in time to see the last gangway removed, and they are now congratulating themselves on having missed the boat.

Mr Norman Craig, KC MP, who booked a passage on the Titanic had actually packed his luggage, but decided at the last moment not to make the journey. 'I had no other conscious reason,' he stated, 'except that in view of the political situation I thought it better to remain at home. I had a providential escape.'

A confession that a dream prevented him from sailing on the Titanic was made yesterday by the Hon. J C Middleton, vice-president of the Akron-Canton Railway of Ohio. Mr Middleton told the dream to his friends, ten days before the tragedy, and this fact is vouched for by several well-known people, one of whom gave Mr Middleton a signed 'affidavit' to that effect.

Mr Middleton says: 'I booked a cabin on the Titanic on March 23. I felt unaccountably depressed at the time, and on April 3 I dreamt that I saw the Titanic capsized in mid-ocean and a lot of the passengers struggling in the water. The following night I dreamt exactly the same dream. The next day I told my wife and several of my friends, and afterwards, on receiving cable advice from America that my business did not necessitate my crossing at once, I decided to cancel my passage.

A fireman named John Coffey, of 12, Sherbourne Terrace in Southampton, joined the Titanic but jumped the ship at Queenstown.

***

During an interview with the *Sunday Independent* for 15 April 1962, the fiftieth anniversary of the disaster, Belfast-born Joseph Mulholland, a former stoker on *Titanic* who was then in his 80th year, and was living in Upton Street, Belfast, stated:

Big Joe is still fond of cats and perhaps he has reason. He recalls that on his way down to the Titanic before she set sail from Belfast with bands playing and crowds cheering, he took pity on a stray cat which was about to have kittens. He brought the cat aboard and put her in a wooden box down in the stoke hold. [He is believed to have named the cat Jenny].

At Southampton, when he was ruminating whether to take on the job of store-keeper on the trip or sign off, another seaman called him over and said: 'Look Big Joe. There's your cat taking its kittens down the gang-plank.'

Joe said: 'That settled it. I went and got my bag and that's the last I saw of the Titanic.'

The following was attributed to the *Irish News* dated 15 April 1998: 'A stoker named Mulholland worked on the Titanic from Belfast to Southampton on the sea trials but was 'influenced' not to continue his voyage when he saw the ship's cat carry each of her kittens down the gang plank onto the quay at Southampton. He thought, 'That cat knows something and has decided that the Titanic is no place for her or her family to spend their lives.'

***

John Henry 'Jack' Stagg (1873–1912) came from a long line of mariners and dock workers, and he was employed as a saloon steward on *Titanic*. When the ship got to Queenstown he posted a letter to his wife, Beatrice, in which he mentioned the near-collision with the SS *New York*: 'I expect you will have heard about the New York breaking away from her moorings because of the suction of our ship. It looked as though there was going to be another collision, but happily the tugs got hold of her in time.'

In a recorded interview in Southampton, his granddaughter, Mrs Jean Fagin, whose mother was Jack's daughter Ivy, stated: 'He always took a little revolver, only a small thing, always beautifully oiled in a little box. He took it on all his voyages to protect himself abroad. But this particular time he told my grandmother to keep it because he wouldn't be needing it on this voyage, and my grandmother felt it was an omen. She used to keep it locked in her trunk, and when the Second World War broke out she took it to the police station when the call went out for firearms.'

Jack lost his life in the sinking, and if his body was found, it was never identified.

***

Southampton-born Arthur Ernest Read Lewis (1884–1973) was a former hotel manager who had been taken on by *Titanic* as a steward. He stated in the *Southampton Echo*, 'The night before the sailing, I asked my wife [Violet] to put my White Star in my cap, and while she was doing it, the star fell all to pieces. With a look of dismay, she said, "I don't like this."'

***

Originally from Edinburgh, John 'Jack' Stewart (1883–1946) was a newly married veranda cafe steward, who had transferred from *Olympic*, and he was on *Titanic* for her delivery trip from Belfast to Southampton. During a recorded interview his daughter, Molly, then Mrs William Adams, stated: 'Mother [Mabel] would never go and see my father off, and this particular day she went and she always swore that that was the most unlucky thing that she ever did.'

Jack survived the disaster. However, he left maritime service and became a driver. He served with the Army Medical Corps during the Great War, and later ran a public house in Southampton with his wife.

***

Gaspare Antonino Pietro 'Luigi' Gatti (1875–1912) was born in Italy and moved to London while he was young. He married Edith Kate Cheese of Chelsea in 1902, and they had one son, Luigi Victor. He had worked on *Olympic* as restaurant manager, being on the ship when it collided with HMS *Hawke*, and transferred to *Titanic* in the same position. Luigi lost his life in the sinking. His body was recovered and he was buried at Fairview Cemetery.

The *Daily Mirror* for 19 April 1912 reported:

> On Sunday night, at about the hour when disaster befell the liner, Mrs Gatti had a strange presentiment of danger, and throughout the night she was unable to sleep. This feeling had such an effect on her that the next morning she came to London and remained with a sister. Mr Gatti held a similar position (restaurant manager) on the Olympic at the time of her collision with the Hawke to that he occupied on the Titanic.

***

The unhappy first marriage of Able Seaman Joe Scarrott, who survived the disaster, had resulted in him committing bigamy, although neither of the women in his life was aware of it. He stated how he was reluctant to go on the journey right up until the ship actually left the dock:

I signed on the articles as 'A B' on Monday, 8 April 1912. The signing on seemed like a dream to me, and I could not believe I had done so, but the absence of my discharge book from my pocket convinced me. When we went to the docks that morning I had so much intention of applying for a job on the Big 'Un as we called her, as I had of going for a trip to the moon. I was assured of as job as Q M on a Union Castle liner, and also I was in low water for 'Bees and honey'. When I went home (36 Albert Road) and told my sister (Elizabeth) what I had done she called me a . . . fool. Now, this was the first and only time that she had shown disapproval of any ship I was going on. In fact, she would not believe me until she found I was minus my discharge book.

I was under orders to join the ship at 7am, Wednesday, 10 April, the time of sailing being 12:00 that morning. It was to be a 'speed up' trip, meaning that we were to go from Southampton to New York, unload, load and back again in 16 days. Although it was unnecessary to take all my kit for this short trip, I did not seem to have the inclination to sort any of it out, and I pondered a lot in my mind whether I should (board) her or give it a miss. Now, in the whole of my 29 years of going to sea I have never had that feeling of hesitation that I experienced then, and I had worked aboard the Titanic when she came to Southampton from the builders, and I had the opportunity to inspect her from stem to stern. This I did, especially the crew quarters, and I must say that she was the finest ship I had ever seen.

On Wednesday 10th, I decided to go, but not with a good heart. Before leaving home I kissed my sister and said 'Goodbye', and as I was leaving she called me back and asked why I had said 'Goodbye' instead of my usual, 'So long, see you again soon.' I told her I had not noticed saying it, neither had I.

On my way to join the ship you can imagine how this incident stuck in my mind. On joining a ship all sailors have much the same routine. You go to your quarters, choose your bunk, and get the gear you require from your bag. Then you change into your uniform. By that time you are called to muster by the chief officer. I took my bag but did not open it, nor did I get into uniform, and I went to muster and fire and boat drill without my uniform. 11:45am: Hands to stations for casting off. I am in the starboard watch, my station is aft, and I am still not in uniform. My actions and manners are the reverse of what they should be. 12:00 noon the order to let go is given.

***

George Barlow was born at Salford in 1872. He was in Southampton to sign on as a first-class bedroom steward. Like numerous members of the *Titanic* crew, he had served on *Olympic*, which was said to be an unlucky vessel, being referred to as a 'ghost ship'. George's father said that when his son was serving as a steward on *Olympic* he was 'frightened' of her, and said 'many times' that he was sure she would sink.

***

Tom Whiteley, a Mancunian who survived the sinking, was described by a newspaper as 'an intelligent young fellow . . . with light hair and blue eyes'. He had just celebrated his 18th birthday on 3 April. He too had previously served on *Olympic* as a steward in the first-class dining saloon. According to the newspaper report, Tom had a foreboding that misfortune would overtake the vessel. Bidding goodbye to some friends at Southampton, he is said to have remarked: 'I don't think I shall ever see you again. We are going to have a wreck.'

***

Another survivor, stewardess Violet Jessop had transferred from *Olympic*. Violet was a devout Roman Catholic, and she always carried a rosary on her person, believing strongly in the power of prayer. She had brought on board a copy of a translated Hebrew prayer that an old Irish woman had given to her, which was supposed to protect her from fire and water. Stewardesses worked as much as seventeen hours a shift and were among the lowest paid on the ship.

***

Jonathan Shepherd served as a junior assistant engineer aboard *Titanic*, and reportedly had an unshakeable fear about joining the liner. He had been on *Olympic* when it collided with HMS *Hawke*. His father was interviewed by the *Northern Daily Telegraph* not long after the sinking and stated that his son was 'down in the dumps' prior to the voyage. When he asked Jonathan 'What are you afraid of? Are you afraid of death?' Jonathan replied, 'No, I'm not afraid of death, but I don't want to go.' His father also stated: 'My lad did not want to go on Titanic, he would rather have stopped on Olympic.'

On the fateful evening, Jonathan helped the ship's engineers to rig pumps inside boiler room number five; however, a slip on a raised access plate led to him breaking his leg. While the leading fireman, Frederick Barrett, and engineer, Herbert Harvey, helped Jonathan to the pump room, the bulkhead breached and he lost his life in the rising water.

7. BAD FOREBODINGS (PASSENGERS)

In his book, published a few months after the disaster, Lawrence Beesley described a kind of out-of-body experience as the disaster unfolded on the liner:

> The curious sense of the whole thing being a dream was very prominent: that all were looking on at the scene from a nearby vantage point in a position of perfect safety, and that those who walked the decks or tied one another's lifebelts on were actors in a scene of which we were but spectators; that the dream would end soon and we should wake up to find the scene had vanished. Many people have had a similar experience in times of danger, but it was very noticeable on the Titanic's deck. I remember observing in particular while tying on a lifebelt for a man on the deck. It is fortunate that it should be so: to be able to survey such a scene dispassionately is a wonderful aid in the destruction of the fears that go with it.

This may have been the result of the shock of being thrown quickly from a feeling of relative safety into a situation of danger, and there are many other similar examples. Walter Dunne, who was the Commissariat Officer at Rorke's Drift during the Zulu War of 1879 (the battle depicted in the film *Zulu!*), remembered that the shock of the news of the disaster at Isandlwana and that a large force of Zulu warriors were on their way to attack the garrison, had a strange effect on him:

> Bromhead and I were resting after luncheon under an awning which we had formed by propping up a tarpaulin with tent poles; everything was peaceful and quiet, when suddenly, we noticed at some distance across the river a large number of mounted natives approaching, preceded by a lot of women and children and oxen. We were going down to find out what they were, but had not gone many steps when we were called

back by one of the men who said that a mounted orderly wished to see the officer in command. Turning back at once we met a mounted man in his shirt sleeves riding hurriedly towards us. His first words were, 'The camp is taken by the Zulus!' When I heard the words a strange feeling which I cannot account for came over me that I had heard this somewhere before. Though we could not realise it fully at first, we soon gathered the truth that a great disaster had befallen that portion of number 3 column which was left to defend the camp at Isandlwana, and that the Zulus, flushed with victory, were advancing to attack our post.

***

W T Stead and an up-and-coming young Irish journalist and dramatist named Shaw Desmond (1877–1960), who shared his interest in spiritualism, were walking together along the Strand in London. Desmond was attempting to discuss an article he was writing for Stead's *Review of Reviews*, but the older man kept steering the conversation back to his own upcoming trip. Stead announced that he would soon be sailing on *Titanic*, a new ship reputed to be unsinkable, and he waxed eloquent on the vessel's size, speed and other outstanding qualities. Desmond, on the other hand, had never heard of *Titanic* before listening to Stead's monologue on the subject.

The two men continued along the Strand together until, at one point, Desmond drew slightly apart from Stead. It was then that an odd feeling suddenly gripped the young journalist, a feeling that he later described as follows: 'There came to me for the first time in my life, but not the last, the conviction of impending death. In this case, that the man at my side would die within a very short time. It was overpowering, and I felt rather helpless, nor did I for a moment associate it with the liner of which he had been speaking.'

Desmond decided not to mention his sudden foreboding of Stead's fate, and the two men eventually went their separate ways. When Desmond arrived home, however, he was astute enough to jot down a brief notation regarding his premonition about Stead, and he dated it 'for future reference'.

It was only a few days later that news of the *Titanic* tragedy reached England. Although there were early rumours that Stead had survived, Desmond felt certain that these were false and that his own premonition about Stead's fate would prove accurate.

'He is not saved,' Desmond told his wife. 'He is drowned.'

***

Major Archibald Butt was military aide to President William Howard Taft, and he was also a close friend of Theodore Roosevelt. When the Republican Party could not decide whether Taft or Roosevelt should be its presidential nominee for the 1912 election, Butt was distressed by his divided loyalties; both nominees were his close friends, and he felt enormous pressure at being caught in the middle of their conflict.

Aware that Major Butt needed to get away from these problems for some much-needed rest, his friend Frank Millet, a noted artist, asked Butt to accompany him to Rome in March. Although Butt accepted the invitation, he immediately felt guilty about 'deserting' the president during a critical time.

In late February Butt wrote a letter to his sister-in-law in which he informed her of his travel plans: 'Don't forget that all my papers are in the storage warehouse, and if the old ship goes down you will find my affairs in shipshape condition.' As an afterthought, he was aware that this statement might alarm her, so he added, 'As I always write you in this way whenever I go anywhere, you will not be bothered by my presentiments now.'

Even though Major Butt attempted to make light of the subject to his sister-in-law, it seems clear that he was in fact having very strong forebodings of some approaching personal danger. Even though his friends attributed his uneasiness to the stress he was under, Butt himself told them that he had 'never had such a peculiar and constant feeling of impending trouble'.

This feeling may have had something to do with what Major Butt did next. In spite of having agreed to accompany Millet to Rome, Butt woke up on 26 February determined to remain in America. He sent wires cancelling all his sailing arrangements, and then he told President Taft what he had done. The president would not hear of Butt's change of plans, however, and insisted that his aide go abroad as originally planned.

Resigned to making the trip to Rome, Butt drew up his will and asked several of the president's Secret Service people to witness it for him. Butt told these men that he had 'an unaccountable feeling that he would encounter some terrible danger before he returned'. A day or two before he left Washington, Butt walked through the White House grounds with a friend, and the two men discussed the major's upcoming trip. Butt told his friend that he 'had the strangest feeling he had ever had in his life that he was to be at the centre of some awful calamity'. Butt said he had had this feeling for several weeks and could not shake it off.

Major Butt sailed for Naples with Frank Millet on 2 March 1912. After delivering messages from President Taft for the pope and the king of Italy, Butt relaxed and tried to build up his strength. Both he and Millet made reservations to return to America when *Titanic* sailed in April.

Although Major Butt's presentiments of danger may have continued throughout his vacation, he seems to have felt that, by booking his passage home on *Titanic*, he would thereby avoid the last possible source of danger his trip might present. Butt told Baron Carlo Allotti that his vacation had been very pleasant, but that he wanted to get back to America in a hurry.

'I'll get to Washington in time,' said the major, 'because I am fortunate enough to have a reservation on the new *Titanic*. When I step aboard the *Titanic*, I shall feel absolutely safe. You know she is unsinkable.'

By the time Butt and Millet arrived in London, however, Butt's presentiments seem to have returned and intensified. A close friend said later that, although usually of a lively and genial temperament, Major Butt was strangely depressed for several days before *Titanic* sailed, so much so that his friends were concerned about him.

'I must go along to see Westminster Abbey,' Butt told them on 9 April, 'because if I miss the abbey now I shall never see it again.'

The *Washington Herald* for 17 April 1912, reported the 'Remarks of the President's Aide before going abroad are Recalled':

President Taft yesterday made earnest efforts to obtain news of Major Archibald Butt, his military aid. He communicated two or three times with the White Star offices in New York, but each time was told that they were sorry to say they could give him no definite information in regard to Major Butt.

The messages received by the President were forwarded by him to Major Butt's sister, in Augusta, and to his brother, Louis Butt, in London. The President was deeply affected by the tragedy, and plainly showed his emotion at yesterday's Cabinet meeting in discussing the appalling loss of life. The President and others have not given up hope for Major Butt, but they acknowledge that the outlook is not bright. While the ordering of the Salem and Chester out to meet the Carpathia was for the purpose of relieving the anxiety of the many sorrowing friends and relatives on shore, the President also had in mind the obtaining of certain news as to whether Major Butt is on the Carpathia.

It was recalled by several of Major Butt's friends here yesterday that just before he left on his trip to Europe he said several times that he had a premonition that 'something terrible' was going to happen. Major Butt made the statement to a newspaper man among others, and added that he couldn't explain it, that he never had had such a feeling before. His friends attributed these remarks to his unstrung nerves, and laughed them off. It was learned yesterday that Major Butt, just before he sailed called three of his friends in and repeating these statements, asked them to witness his will.

***

Arthur Gee (1865–1912) was a Salfordian in his late-forties. He was the son of a calico dyer, and he had studied the chemistry of calico printing in Germany. A multilinguist, he had apparently organised a trip across the Atlantic to take a job as manager of a linen mill near Mexico City, after which he was contemplating retiring. His first-class ticket cost him nearly £40. He intended to sail from Liverpool, but because industrial unrest had affected the port there the ship was delayed and, as fate would have it, he happily agreed to travel to Southampton to board the brand new luxury liner RMS *Titanic*.

His dog had acted strangely on the day he made his way to the station, as if it sensed foreboding and was trying to warn him not to get on the train. His local newspaper at Lytham in Lancashire reported: 'He kept a dog, which usually reserved its most affectionate demonstrations for Mr Gee's children. Mr Gee, in the course of his business, made frequent journeys from home, but his going and comings were apparently regarded with unconcern by the dog. On the occasion of his departure to embark at Southampton, however, the dog followed the cab to the railway station, and at the station jumped about Mr Gee in so demonstrative a fashion that he remarked on the strangeness of the incident to a friend who was seeing him off, and said how remarkable it was that the dog should appear to know that he was going on a long voyage.'

A survivor named Algernon Barkworth recorded: 'Jones and Gee were looking over the side . . . Jones and Gee were standing by, with arms on the rail, looking down. I imagine they were preparing for death.'

Arthur was reported to be a strong swimmer but he drowned in the sinking. His body was number 275 recovered from the water by the *Mackay-Bennett*, being described as aged about 60, although he was actually 47, having dark hair and a moustache. He was wearing a brown overcoat, with a tuxedo suit and dress pants. His effects were a silver watch, gold chain, silver cigarette case, various small items and some banknotes.

His eldest brother, Walter, who had stayed on in Moscow as manager of the calico works, died at about the same time as *Titanic* was lost. Arthur's remains arrived in New York and were transported to Liverpool on *Baltic*. His funeral took place at St John's Church, on the Height in Salford near Manchester, and he was buried in the grave next to his father. The gravestone stood for some time but has now been removed and the area has been grassed over.

***

James Hainsworth Ismay (1867–1930), the younger brother of Bruce Ismay, lived at Iwerne Minster House in Iwerne Minster near Shaftesbury in Dorset. He was a partner in the White Star Line from 1891, but he never really had much interest in shipping and preferred to concentrate on agriculture.

Some years after the disaster one of his grandchildren stated: 'I once asked my grandmother [Muriel] why my grandfather was not on the Titanic. She told me he was to have been, but had very serious pneumonia so was at home. She then added that on the night of the Titanic disaster he suddenly came out of the coma and said, "Bruce is in trouble! Bruce is in trouble!"'

The anti-establishment London newspaper *Reynold's* of 21 April 1912 reported on the Ismay family under the title 'A Survivor of the Titanic':

In this column, where as a rule we write only of the living, we may speak of Joseph Bruce Ismay. Mr Ismay, who is in his fiftieth year, was born in Liverpool. He is chairman and managing director of the White Star Line. He is president and member of the British committee of the International Mercantile Marine Company, which was incorporated in 1893 under the laws of New Jersey. He is also, with several other company associations, a director of the London and North-Western Railway. But it is more to our present purpose to say that he is one of the survivors of the Titanic.

Ismay is a rare name. We fancy it is not to be found anywhere outside the north-west of England. It was the name of a lady living in the time of King Edward I, who is claimed as an ancestress of Mr Ismay. The first to make the name widely known was Mr Ismay's father, the late Thomas Henry Ismay, who, coming out of Maryport in Cumberland, became a shipping prince in Liverpool. It was in 1868 that he established, in conjunction with William Imrie, the company which has since become famous as the White Star Line. It was for him that was built the first vessel to have her saloon accommodation mid-ships.

Joseph Bruce Ismay is the eldest of three brothers, and appears to be the only one who is actively associated with shipping. He has two sons and two daughters, his wife being the eldest daughter of George R Sokieffelin of New York. His youngest brother, Charles Bowen, married her sister. The other brother, James Hainsworth Ismay, married into the English aristocracy. He is now lying seriously ill with pneumonia at Iwerne Minster House in Dorsetshire. One of the sisters is the wife of Mr Geoffrey Drags, who used to be MP for Derby.

Joseph Bruce Ismay is an Old Harrovian; shoots, motors and golfs; and is a member of the Reform Club. He has a house at Thurstaston on the Dee near Birkenhead, another at Mossley Hill in Liverpool, and another in Hill Street. There are plenty of Hill Streets, but the one we mean is the fashionable street which runs out of Berkeley Square, a street where only 'nobs' live.

***

Stephen Curnow Jenkin (1879–1912), a native of St Ives in Cornwall, was a miner who had moved to live in Michigan in 1903, and in the summer of 1911 he travelled back to St Ives to visit his family. He was booked to go back to America on another ship, but because of the coal strikes he was switched to *Titanic*.

It was reported that soon after leaving St Ives for Southampton he had misgivings about the new ship and returned to his parents' house in St Ives to leave his valuables (including his watch) with them, in case anything should happen to him. He sent three picture postcards of *Titanic* to his parents from Southampton, Cherbourg and Queenstown. Stephen died in the sinking and if his body was recovered, it was never identified.

***

South-African-born teenager Edith Eileen Brown (1896–1997) was travelling with her parents, Thomas and Elizabeth. Thomas died in the sinking but Elizabeth survived. They were in the hotel business and were on their way to make a new life in America. She later stated: 'Then we went up the gangway and then my father took the bag like, you know, so my mother turned around and asked if he was ill and he said no he was quite alright. Because he had a premonition before he left South Africa, but he wouldn't tell my mother what it was . . . then there was a boat called the *New York* and she nearly went into the *Titanic* . . . my father said, when he saw that, he said that's a bad omen.'

Edith married Frederick Haisman in 1917, and they had ten children. She had become a centenarian when she died in a Southampton nursing home as one of the longest-surviving victims of the *Titanic* disaster.

***

A girl named Lois Brown (later Jacobs) had been let out of school at Woolston in Southampton, not far from the docks, and under the supervision of a teacher she and her classmates watched *Titanic*, 'come out so far and then there was a delay and it was drawn back in again to the wharf, and so we waited and waited and finally they started again and that time she went down out of sight in the Southampton waters'.

A man standing nearby on the quay stated that it was a sign of bad luck that the ship had backed up, but probably having seen that his remarks had upset the children he tried to lighten the situation he had caused, by saying, 'Let's hope not.'

***

Edith Corse Evans was a first-class passenger returning to New York after a trip to Europe, along with three married sisters, Charlotte Appleton (1848–1924), Caroline Brown (1852–1928), and Malvina Helen Cornell (1856–1941), who were returning to America after attending the funeral of their sister, Lady Elizabeth Drummond (1849–1912), who had died in Paris. The sisters knew Colonel Archibald Gracie IV. During the voyage Edith told the colonel that a fortune teller had once warned her to 'beware of water', and she was convinced that there was some truth in the prophecy. Despite the warning, various accounts state that Edith gave up a seat in the last lifeboat to leave *Titanic* to Caroline Brown, stating, 'You go first. You have children waiting for you at home.' She was one of four first-class female passengers to lose her life in the disaster.

***

George Washington Vanderbilt II (1862–1914) intended to travel with his wife Edith. Their footman, Bath-born Edwin Charles Wheeler (1886–1912), had actually loaded their belongings onto *Titanic* two days prior to travelling, when a family member warned them not to travel on the ship, stating: 'So many things can go wrong on a maiden voyage'. They heeded the warning and decided to travel on RMS *Olympic* instead, while Edwin chose to (or was asked to) accompany the Vanderbilt's luggage. He and the luggage went down with the ship.

Alfred Gwynne Vanderbilt (1877–1915) was a multi-millionaire sportsman and heir to the Vanderbilt shipping and railroad empire. He was returning from a trip to Europe, and cancelled his passage on *Titanic* so late that some early newspaper accounts listed him as being on board. He lived on to become one of the celebrated casualties of the sinking of *Lusitania* three years later.

***

Just after the incident concerning SS *New York* in Southampton harbour, Renee Harris (1876–1969) reported that a handsome stranger approached her and, after intimating that the incident was a bad omen, he asked her if she 'loved life'. When she replied in the affirmative, the man reportedly said, 'Then you will get off this ship at Cherbourg, if we get that far. That's what I'm going to do.' The man apparently kept good his statement as she never saw him again.

Renee was the wife of the theatre producer, Henry Birkhardt Harris (1866–1912), who had stepped back out of a lifeboat to make room for some women and children; a brave act that cost him his life. Renee decided to carry on his work and became New York's first female theatre producer.

***

Nora Agnes Keane was a 47-year-old from County Limerick who had lived in Pennsylvania since 1888, where she worked as a housekeeper. She had been on an extended visit to her family in Ireland and was on her way back to America. She had intended to return on an earlier boat but believed that she would be more comfortable on *Titanic*. During the voyage she confessed to Edwina Trout, one of the women she shared a cabin with, that she had a terrible foreboding that the ship would sink. The explanation for this seems to be that as she was on the tender bringing her out from Queenstown to board *Titanic* she dropped her prayer book and rosary beads into the sea, which, being a very superstitious woman she took to be a bad omen. She survived the sinking and eventually returned to Ireland, where she died in 1944 from complications after suffering a fractured hip.

***

W Rex Sowden was a captain in charge of the Salvation Army Corps in the town of Kirkcudbright, Scotland. On the evening of 14 April 1912, Sowden had already retired for the night when someone knocked on his door and asked, 'Will you please come at once, Captain. Jessie Sayre is dying.'

Captain Sowden dressed himself immediately and went to the room of the little orphan girl in question. He sat alone with the dying child for a few minutes, but at precisely eleven o'clock Jessie sat upright in her bed. When she noticed Sowden sitting at her bedside, she said, 'Hold my hand, Captain. I am so afraid. Can't you see that big ship sinking in the water?'

Thinking that the child's mind was wandering, Captain Sowden sought to comfort her by saying that she had only been having a bad dream. But little Jessie was not to be comforted.

'No,' she replied, 'the ship is sinking. Look at all those people who are drowning. Someone called Wally is playing a fiddle and coming to you.'

Sowden looked around the room but saw nothing unusual. He laid the little girl back into her bed, and she then lapsed into a coma.

Captain Sowden sat with the dying child for several hours and observed no change in her condition, but then, suddenly, he heard the sound of the latch on the bedroom door. Arising, Sowden went to the door and opened it, but saw nobody there. However, he had the distinct sensation that someone passed by him and entered the bedroom. Sowden rushed back to Jessie's bed and saw that a change had occurred, and that death was only moments away. The little girl suddenly opened her eyes and said that her mother had come 'to take me to heaven'. Sowden held Jessie's hand for a moment, and the child then died peacefully.

Captain Sowden rose from the bedside and was preparing to go for help when he again heard the lifting of the latch on the bedroom door. Again Sowden opened the door to find no one visible, but he couldn't help coming to the inescapable conclusion that 'the mother had departed with her child'.

According to Rex Sowden, 'Some hours later, the whole world was startled by the tragedy of the Titanic. Among those drowned was Wally Hartley, its bandmaster, whom I knew well as a boy. I had no knowledge of his going to sea or having anything to do with any ship.'

In later years, when thinking about the little girl's vision of the sinking ship, Captain Sowden said, 'What I thought was hallucination was a vision that stamped itself indelibly on my brain and changed my whole spiritual outlook.'

Wallace Hartley lived at Colne in Lancashire until he was aged 15, which was when Rex Sowden said he knew him. After the Great War, Sowden lived at Newcastle upon Tyne, from where he toured the country as a well-known clairvoyant and 'noted trance medium'.

***

Isaac Frauenthal (1868–1932) was a lawyer living in New York. In March 1912 he travelled to Europe to attend the wedding of his brother, Henry, in Nice. The two brothers decided to return to America on *Titanic*'s maiden voyage and travelled to Southampton to board the great liner on 10 April.

After *Titanic* had set sail, Isaac told his brother and new sister-in-law of an occurrence that had made him uneasy. Before boarding *Titanic* he had had a dream. As he described it, 'It seemed to me that I was on a big steamship which suddenly crashed into something and began to go down. I saw in the dream as vividly as I could see with open eyes the gradual settling of the ship, and I heard the cries of frightened passengers.'

He seems to have regarded this dream as a simple nightmare, but then he had the identical dream a second time.

'I didn't pay much attention to the first dream,' he said later, 'but when it was repeated I must confess I became a little worried.'

When Isaac told Henry and his wife about the two dreams, they laughed and made light of his worries. This may have relieved Isaac's uneasiness a bit, for he later commented on the atmosphere aboard *Titanic*: 'I don't suppose any ship that ever took an Atlantic track had a happier, more confident crowd of passengers than the Titanic. The novelty of having a part in the maiden trip of the world's greatest ship appealed to everybody. Then, too, nearly all of us felt that there was no reason to be alarmed or apprehensive about anything.'

On the night of 14 April, Isaac was lying in bed reading when he heard a long, drawn-out 'rubbing noise'. He got up to investigate and, hearing that *Titanic* had struck something, went to awaken his brother. Henry did not think that the situation was at all serious and returned to bed. Isaac later admitted, 'I wasn't sure, having that dream in mind, so made for the deck, looking for Captain Smith or any other officer who could tell me what really happened.'

Reaching the deck, he overheard Captain Smith advise John Jacob Astor to awaken his wife, as the passengers might have to take to the lifeboats. Hearing this, Isaac returned to his brother's stateroom and again pounded on the door. So great was the general confidence in

Titanic, however, that he had great difficulty in conveying to Henry that there was real danger.

When Henry and his wife finally arrived on deck, Isaac said, 'Well, Henry, I wasn't so foolish, was I?'

'Oh,' his brother replied, 'the boat is too big. It can't sink.'

Mrs Frauenthal was put into a lifeboat, while Henry and Isaac remained on deck. As the lifeboat began to lower, Henry's wife threatened to jump out of the boat if her husband did not join her. On impulse the two brothers jumped down into the lifeboat, and all three Frauenthals were saved.

***

Eugene Daly, a young Irishman from Athlone, boarded *Titanic* at Queenstown along with a group of friends who were also travelling in steerage. It wasn't long before young Mr Daly told of having had a disturbing dream, and his friend Bertha Mulvihill later recalled the incident.

'It was a funny thing,' said Miss Mulvihill. 'There was a boy named Eugene Daly from my home town who was with us. When we left Queenstown he told us he had dreamt that the Titanic was going to sink. And every night we were at sea he told us he had dreamt that the Titanic was going down before we reached New York. On Sunday night, just before he went to bed, he told us that the Titanic was going to sink that night. It was uncanny.'

Elsewhere, Miss Mulvihill related how Daly knew the ship would sink because, in his dream, 'he had plainly seen the collision with the iceberg'.

After *Titanic*'s collision with the iceberg, Miss Mulvihill stood on the slanting deck as the last lifeboat began to be lowered away. A sailor in the boat looked at the young woman and cried, 'Jump!' She did, and landed safely in the lifeboat.

Daly was one of the few male steerage passengers who were fortunate enough to survive the sinking of *Titanic*.

A newspaper reporter quoted Miss Mulvihill as saying that Eugene 'Ryan' was the person who had experienced the premonitory dreams about the *Titanic* disaster, but her grandson has assured me that she was actually talking about Eugene Daly.

8. 'DEATH IS THE GATE OF LIFE'

Edward John Smith, captain of *Titanic*, was born in the 'Potteries' district of Hanley in Stoke-on-Trent on 27 January 1850. His father, also named Edward, worked in the local trade as a potter, and his mother was named Catherine. They later took over a shop.

Captain Smith joined the White Star Line in 1880. Although he became respected in his profession, his safety record was not good, being involved in five incidents before he was appointed to *Titanic*.

Having been appointed to RMS *Coptic* in 1889, in December of the following year he grounded her in Rio de Janeiro. In 1899 he ran RMS *Republic* aground off the Sandy Hook Peninsula in New Jersey, and put RMS *Adriatic* on a sandbank in the Ambrose Channel near New York in 1899. He hit a tug boat in New York Harbour, and soon afterwards, on 21 September 1911, he was captain of RMS *Olympic* when she was rammed by the warship HMS *Hawke*.

Several months before the disaster, Captain Smith had spoken about his bad luck at sea with a businessman named J P Grant, stating that he felt that he had been jinxed, and said that he would resign if he had another accident in a liner.

There have been various accounts of Captain Smith's last moments concerning the disaster, and it is almost certain that if his distinctive body and uniform was found, it would have been identified; which it was not. Harold Bride was the junior wireless officer on the ship, and part of his testimony to the United States inquiry when questioned by Senator William Alden Smith went as follows:

Senator Smith: 'When did you last see the captain? When he told you to take care of yourself?'

Mr Bride: 'The last I saw of the captain he went overboard from the bridge, sir.'

Senator Smith: 'Did you see the Titanic sink?'

Mr Bride: 'Yes, sir.'

Senator Smith: 'And the captain was at that time on the bridge?'

Mr Bride: 'No, sir.'

Senator Smith: 'What do you mean by overboard?'

Mr Bride: 'He jumped overboard from the bridge when we were launching the collapsible lifeboat.'

Senator Smith: 'I should judge from what you have said that this was about three or four minutes before the boat sank?'

Mr Bride: 'Yes. It would be just about five minutes before the boat sank.'

Senator Smith: 'About five minutes?'

Mr Bride: 'Yes.'

Senator Smith: 'Do you know whether the captain had a life belt on?'

Mr Bride: 'He had not when I last saw him.'

Senator Smith: 'He had not?'

Mr Bride: 'No, sir.'

Senator Smith: 'Did the bridge go under water at about the same time?'

Mr Bride: 'Yes, sir. The whole of the ship was practically under water to the forward funnel, and when I saw her go down the stern came out of the water and she slid down fore and aft.'

Senator Smith: 'The captain at no time went over until the vessel sank?

Mr Bride: 'No, sir.'

Senator Smith: 'He went with the vessel?

Mr. Bride: 'Practically speaking; yes, sir.'

At least three eyewitnesses, a passenger named Charles Eugene Williams, in lifeboat 14, and two crew members named Harry Senior and Walter 'Wally' Hurst, both in collapsible B, say they saw the captain in the water as the lifeboats were trying to get away from the liner, and Williams said he actually had a short conversation with him. Can all three of them be wrong?

A few months later, Captain Peter Pryal of Baltimore, who was a lifelong friend and had sailed with him, was certain he met Edward Smith walking the streets of that city. The usual explanation is that it was simply a case of mistaken identity, but is there any possibility that it could have really been Captain Smith?

The *Daily Sketch* for 30 April 1912, reported, under the heading 'His last Act Was to Save a Child's Life – Refused to get into a Boat':

Of all the wild and irresponsible messages that were sent to this country in the first hours following the sinking of the Titanic the one that caused the grief to Englishmen was the statement that Captain Smith had committed suicide on the bridge of his ship. That statement was quickly contradicted. It was proved that Captain Smith died like a sailor, but the exact manner of his death was not described. Many eyewitnesses have testified to seeing the captain on the bridge as the great liner was engulfed, and others say they saw the officer dive from the bridge just before the ship sank, but according to an interview published in the *New York World* Captain Smith died the greatest of all deaths. His last act was to save the life of a child.

The story is told by Charles Eugene Williams, coach of the Harrow Racquet Club, who was one of those saved from the Titanic. Mr Williams is the guest of Mr George E Standing, and the latter gave the *New York World* reporter the account as told to him by Mr Williams.

'He is a good swimmer [Charles Williams],' said Mr Standing, 'and went overboard with a life preserver when he couldn't stay on deck any longer. He was in the icy water for over two hours before he was finally hauled into one of the lifeboats. He says that he saw Captain Smith swimming around in the icy water with an infant in his arms and a lifebelt. When the small boat went to his rescue Captain Smith handed them the child, but refused to get in himself.

'He did ask what had become of First Officer Murdoch. We told him Murdoch had blown his brains out with a revolver. Then Captain Smith

79

pushed himself away from the lifeboat, threw his lifebelt from him and slowly sank from sight. He did not come to the surface again.'

It may be stated that there is no official confirmation that Mr Murdoch shot himself: we give the whole account as it appeared in the *New York World*.

Mr Williams' story is borne out by Harry Senior, a fireman of the Titanic who arrived on the Lapland on Sunday. In interviews for the *New York Times* on 19 April 1912, and the *Illustrated London News* for 4 May 1912, Senior said: 'The ship was pretty near sinking then, and the captain shouted, "Each man for himself". I had noticed him on the bridge before that. He was pacing up and down sending up rockets and giving orders.

'It is a dirty lie to say that such a man as he shot himself.

'When the Captain's order came Senior dived over the side.

'As I was swimming to the boat I saw the captain in the water. He was swimming with a baby in his arms, raising it out of the water as he swam on his back.

'He swam to a boat, put the baby in, and then swam back to the ship. I also had picked up a baby, but it died from the cold before I could reach the boat.'

Walter 'Wally' Hurst and his father-in-law, William Mintram, served as firemen on the ship. They met each other shortly before *Titanic* went down. William had a life jacket and he gave it to his son-in-law. This act of courage probably cost William his life, and may well have contributed to the fact that Walter was able to stay on the upturned collapsible B and survive.

His daughter, Rosina (later Broadbere) related: 'My father was one of the last ones off and he was in the collapsible boat that was upside down in the water, he was on the top of that, and he always said that, you know the captain of the ship, they say all sorts of things about what happened to him, well he said somebody swam up to the boat and he couldn't get on because there was so many on there, and he said "Good luck, boys" and he went. My dad swore it was the captain that said that.'

It is believed that a survivor was picked up by *Carpathia* and seemingly rushed away from the eyes of those around him. Who was this man? Some suggest it was Bruce Ismay, the chairman and managing director of the White Star Line. However, at least one passenger, Jack Thayer, was allowed to go into his cabin and speak to him, so what would have been the point of getting him away from the others and then let them see him? It is also known that the survivors of the crew were not disembarked with the passengers, but were taken by a tender, the *George Starr*, to Pier 61. There seems to have been an attempt to keep the crew away from awkward questions until they had been briefed. The root of all evil also raised its head. According to the *London Daily News*, one of the things the Senate inquiry intended to find out was: 'Why a Marconi company's official sent a wireless to the operator on the *Carpathia* on Thursday, stating: "Say nothing. Hold your story for dollars in four figures."'

If it was Captain Smith on *Carpathia*, surely the people who were rescued in the same lifeboat as him would have recognised him and remembered? However, it was too dark to distinguish faces, and in fact, Jane Hoyt, who had been in collapsible A, stated later that she did not even realise until they reached *Carpathia* that her husband Frederick had been one of four men rescued by collapsible D when it returned to the wreckage, and he was in the same boat as her when she was picked up by it. Was one of the other three men Captain Smith?

It is suggested that Charles Williams had been in the water for two hours before he got into lifeboat 14, from where he spoke to Captain Smith. Based on this evidence, Smith must have been in the water as long as Williams, and after being in the icy water for such a long time, would Smith have been in any conscious state to say who he was? Two of his senior crew, 5th Officer Harold Lowe and Leading Fireman Tom Threlfall, were in the boat, but Lowe was preoccupied organising the rescue attempt and Threlfall was busy looking after one of the female passengers.

In addition to the darkness, and the dreadful condition of the people in the boats, there was a lot of confusion. Lifeboat 14 had met up with Lifeboats 4, 10, 12 and Collapsible D. Officer Lowe decided that his boat should return to the site of the wreck to try to rescue survivors. He began to transfer all the passengers out of Lifeboat 14 into the other lifeboats in the group.

Tom Threlfall recalled: 'Then he (Officer Lowe) called to several other boats close by, "Throw out your painters," and we linked them all up. Mr Lowe passed about fifty women and children from his boat, and said, 'We will go for the wreckage', to which other people were clinging. From the wreckage we picked up four men. Then Mr Lowe called out, 'There's a boat over there and she's sinking [collapsible A]'. Although we were then towing a collapsible boat [D] with about eighty people in her we reached the sinking boat just as the water was up to her gunwale and took twenty-six men and one woman, a Mrs [Rhoda Mary "Rosa"] Abbott, off her. I held the woman in my arms till we reached *Carpathia*.

On 23 July 1912, numerous newspapers around the world reported 'Titanic Mystery – Captain Smith said to be in Hiding'.

Peter Pryal, veteran captain of Montreal, and a long-time friend of Captain Smith, of the *Titanic*, swears that Captain Smith was not drowned. Pryal declares that he saw him recently in Baltimore. Captain Smith tried to evade him by taking the train bound for Washington. It is stated that Captain Smith's nephew, a resident of Baltimore, disappeared the day after his uncle's re-appearance.

Captain Peter Pryal (says the New York correspondent of the *Daily Telegraph*, on 21 July), one of the oldest mariners of Baltimore, well-known in shipping circles, who sailed with Captain Smith of the Titanic when the latter was commander of the Majestic, made a startling statement yesterday. He had seen and talked to Captain Smith on Friday at Baltimore and St Paul Streets.

He declares that he walked up to Captain Smith and said, 'Captain Smith, how are you?' Then, according to Captain Pryal, the man answered, 'Very well, Pryal; but please don't detain me. I'm on business.' Captain Pryal says he followed the man, and saw him buy a ticket for Washington, and as he passed through the gate of the railroad station he turned, recognised Pryal again, and remarked, 'Be proud, shipmate, until we meet again.'

'There's no possibility of my being mistaken,' said Captain Pryal yesterday. 'I have known Captain Smith too long. I know him even without his beard. I firmly believe that he was saved, and in some mysterious manner brought to the United States. I am willing to swear to my statement.'

Captain Pryal is a plain citizen, a teetotaller and a churchgoer, and one of the last men, it is believed, to desire publicity. He realises the incredulity his statement will awaken. 'People will say I'm either a second-sight man or insane: but they are mistaken. I simply believe the evidence of my eyes and ears.'

Dr Warfield of Baltimore vouches that Captain Pryal is perfectly sane.

Captain Smith had a distinctive look, and Captain Pryal actually spoke to the man. Could it really have been a case of misidentification of both visual and voice?

Was it a coincidence that a man who was a long-time friend saw him after the disaster in a region of the United States associated with his stepfamily? Smith's mother, Catherine (nee Marsh, 1808–93), had married George John Hancock on 13 March 1831, but he died in about 1847. She then married Edward Smith (1804–1864), Captain Smith's father. In consequence of this, Smith had half siblings named Joseph, John and Thirza (or Thirra) Hancock. Joseph had at least two sons named George John (born in 1858), and Frank Arthur Douglas (born in 1862), and Captain Smith confirms in a letter of 1905 that Frank was his nephew, and was an obvious favourite of his. Frank was originally married to Annie Oaks Hatch, with whom he had eleven children, and after her death he remarried and had three children. He moved to the United States, where he lived in Savannah, New York, and had an office in the city. In the letter Captain Smith remarks, 'I gather Frank and family moved up to CT from Savannah.' The Hancock family were also known to have been associated with Baltimore and Washington DC, Captain Smith's destination on the train.

Were at least four men mistaken? Or could it be that Captain Edward Smith was rescued in one of Officer Lowe's group of lifeboats, and being the captain of *Titanic* – 'The captain goes down with his ship' – which had taken a lot of their loved ones to the bottom of the ocean, was he taken away from the midst of the rescued passengers on *Carpathia* to avoid facing any awkward questions or even hostility?

If it was Captain Smith who was seen in Baltimore, why did he not make it known that he had survived? The captain of a ship is the most responsible person on board the vessel and his primary role is to get all the passengers to their destination in safety. With this in mind, it could have been Bruce Ismay who ordered that he stayed quiet until they judged the reaction of the authorities and the general public. They were aware that there would be an inquiry which would not be sympathetic towards Smith; probably being prosecuted if they thought he was still alive. Indeed, Ismay came into severe criticism, and was even attacked. It was stated that Smith and Ismay had agreed to increase speed even though they had been warned of dangerous ice floes in the region. When the inquiry found that Smith was guilty of negligence, he probably decided not to speak out. He was aged 62 and had stated that he was ready for retirement, and as time went by it became more and more unethical to disclose his whereabouts – and a lot safer to stay silent.

In her 1912 book *There Are No Dead*, Madame Sophie de Meissner, an American spiritualist, stated that Captain Smith spoke to her from the other side on the afternoon of 20 April 1912. Captain Smith, testified, saying, '*I* was responsible, though I could not have averted the accident! I was running too fast, though even if I had been running slower the effect would have been the same. We collided in such a way that the ship was ripped open all her length, and if we had been going slower she would have passed (in) the very same way over the sunken flow that was her death. She could not have stopped even had she been going slowly. The fault was in the ship.

No ship of such size is proper to send where there are icebergs. This is my witness . . . Amen.'

The ship, of course, was not ripped open all her length. De Meissner also states that on reading to the captain the contents of Lord Mersey's report, he replied:

> I don't see how I could have done otherwise than as I did. I had done it hundreds of times before and nothing had ever happened. Every captain who crosses the ocean does it. It is wrong of course but then it is the custom. Could we know such terrible conditions as had never been known before prevailed? As I said before, those long ships are too unwieldy to use in crossing the ocean or in any other place. Tell them if they use them again there will be just such another accident and they must give them up. No other ship must be built of the size of 'Titanic'. It will be fatal to many more people than were lost on her. I insist upon your publishing this. It is most important. That is all. Smith – late captain of Titanic.

Captain Smith's widow, Sarah Eleanor (nee Pennington), was knocked down by a taxi in London on 1 May 1931, aged 69, and died of her injuries in hospital. She was buried at Brookwood Cemetery in Woking. Their daughter, Helen Melville, gave birth to twins named Simon and Priscilla. Simon was a flying officer aged just 20 when he was killed in action on 23 March 1944, while serving with the Royal Air Force during the Second World War; and Priscilla died in Scotland from polio aged 23, on 7 October 1947. Helen died in Oxford on 18 August 1973, aged 75, and was buried with her mother.

***

The *Washington Herald* for 19 April 1912 carried an account by Mrs Churchill Candee of Washington, in which she stated:

> The action of men of the Titanic was noble. They stood back in every instance that I noticed, and gave the women and children the first chance to get away safely.
>
> Particularly heroic was the conduct of Isidor Straus, Major Archibald Butt, John Jacob Astor and Henry B Harris. They formed a group. Most of the passengers were on the stern of Titanic, for the leak was forward and it was known that if she sank it would be bow first.

An officer of *Titanic* ordered Mrs Straus into a boat. She said, 'I will not leave my husband. We've been together all these years and I'll not leave him now.'

It brought tears to our eyes to witness her great devotion for her husband. Major Butt was one of God's own noblemen. I saw him working desperately to get the women and children into the boats. What need can there be of recounting the heroic deeds performed by those men who remained on Titanic? To dwell upon them only sickens the heart with the realisation of how they perished.

Madame de Meissner held a séance in which she was reported as stating that she made contact with Major Archibald Butt:

13 July 1912 – Titanic Victims – Alleged Spirit Messages
A strange incident, an outcome of the Titanic disaster, was brought to light this morning by the publication of a message, addressed to President Taft, purporting to come from the late Major Archibald Butt, who was one of the Titanic victims. This alleged communication from the spirit world was delivered through the non-professional mediumship of Madame de Meissner. The message is of considerable length, and much of it is purely personal to the President.

According to Madame de Meissner, the communication came to her on April 18, a few hours before the Carpathia got in touch with New York, after having reached the Titanic's survivors. At that time the President was making every effort to assure himself of the safety of his friend, Major Butt.

'I want so much to speak to someone in the world,' runs Madame de Meissner's record of Major Butt's message. 'I want to get a message through to the President; I mean Taft. I have never felt more entirely and unutterably happy than I do at this moment, every care I ever had has slipped from me, and I only feel thankful that I could do a little to help those who were so terrified. I only wish I could have done more.

A description of the last moments of consciousness in this, and the first moment of consciousness in the 'other world' is a further feature of the communication which Madame de Meissner transcribed and transmitted to President Taft. According to Madame de Meissner, she received a message almost immediately after the tragedy from Mr William T Stead, who was a member of the English Society for Psychical Research, and who had been in correspondence with Madame de Meissner for some time before booking his passage on the Titanic.

***

Testimonies from *Titanic*'s survivors commented on the stoic and contemplative way that Stead faced his fate as he sat in the first-class smoking room patiently reading a book as the tragic events unfolded all around him, as if his death was inevitable. Mrs William Shelley, who left on the ship's final lifeboat, reflected on watching his 'prayerful attitude, or one of profound meditation', and a New York lawyer, Frederick Seward, remarked on Stead's 'beautiful composure', concluding that 'he faced death with philosophic calm'.

Newspapers in early November 1913 reported under the heading: 'From the Other World; W T Stead Appears to a Friend: Explains His Sensations':

General, Sir Alfred Edward Turner KCB, will tell for the first time in a book now on the eve of publication the connected story of Mr W T Stead's appearance to him at his residence, Carlyle House, Chelsea Embankment.

'The first manifestation of Mr Stead, within a week of the Titanic disaster, occurred in this very room. Probably the first manifestation was a shadow seen on a glass, but I am speaking now of the audible voice on an occasion subsequently.

'I went to Cambridge House in Wimbledon, Mr Stead's home, and there, at a miscellaneous circle . . . Mr Stead appeared twice, at my right shoulder. The appearances were short and transient, not exactly flashes – more than that – but they rapidly faded. But the voice was very well heard.'

'And what did the voice say, Sir Alfred?'

'I am very happy to be with you again,' was the first words of greeting.

'When the *Titanic* sank, there was for myself a very short, sharp struggle to regain breath, and I came to my senses – it seemed in an instant – surrounded by hundreds of beings who, like myself, had passed over to a new existence, but were utterly unable to realise what had happened. They were quite unconscious of the fact that they were not still in the flesh. They were groping about in obscurity and uncertainty, and I set myself at once to do missionary work by enlightening the people as to what had happened and what was their new condition.'

As a point of interest it has been reported: 'It was Mr Stead who revealed the fact that the hymn *Nearer, My God, to Thee* was a favourite with King Edward. Mr Stead had hit upon the idea of publishing a work *Hymns That Have Helped*, and it contained *Nearer, My God, to Thee*, and there was a note attached that the then Prince of Wales had been appealed to for an opinion as to a hymn which had helped him most. Mr Stead received a reply from the Prince to the effect that while he had not made a special study of hymns, the one *Nearer, My God, to Thee* had interest to him.'

RMS *Olympic* (left) and RMS *Titanic* (right) were sister ships of the Olympic class of liners built in Belfast. Several of the crew of *Olympic* considered her to be an unlucky ship, and their fears did not fade when they were transferred to *Titanic*.

Captain Edward Smith was said to have been seen alive after the *Titanic* disaster by a man who had sailed with him, known him for many years, and actually spoke to him that day. Could it really have been a case of misidentification of both visual and voice?

The Amen-Ra coffin lid was believed to have been cursed and brought misfortune to all who had anything to do with it; including staff at the British Museum where it was on show in the Egyptian Room. According to a newspaper report rediscovered by the author, to try to break the curse a copy was made and displayed in its place, while the original was purchased by an American Egyptologist and deliberately secreted among the cargo aboard *Titanic*, bound for New York.

Morgan Andrew Robertson was an American short story writer who published a book in 1898 entitled *Futility*, which in many ways mirrored the *Titanic* disaster. It was reissued in 1912 after *Titanic* sank under the title *The Wreck of the Titan*. Robertson was found dead in a hotel three years after the disaster; with his body standing upright.

Chief Officer Henry Tingle Wilde was unexpectedly transferred from *Olympic* to *Titanic*. He lamented to his sister, 'I still don't like this ship ... I have a queer feeling about it.' Henry lost his life in the sinking, and if his body was recovered, it was never identified.

Benjamin, Eva and Esther Hart. Esther was of the opinion that those who said *Titanic* was unsinkable were throwing in the face of God. She felt 'dread and uneasiness' throughout the trip, and would not sleep during the dark hours. Esther and Eva survived the sinking but Ben did not.

The three Southampton-born Slade brothers named Alfred Edward, Bertram and Thomas, became apprehensive about working on *Titanic* after one of them had a bad dream about the ship. Fortunately, they arrived at the dock too late to board her and missed the doomed voyage.

Just after the incident concerning SS *New York* in Southampton harbour, Renee Harris reported that a handsome stranger approached her and, after intimating that the incident was a bad omen, he tried to warn her to get off the ship at Cherbourg; which apparently he did, as she never saw him again.

Newspapers reported on 4 March 1913:

W T Stead in Spirit Life
On Sunday morning, in the Hyde Park (Sydney) Unitarian Church, Rev.
George Walters delivered a discourse on the alleged messages from
W T Stead from Borderland. The preacher said he was not concerned
with the multitudinous instances in which so-called mediums in
various parts of the world had professed to give oral messages from
the departed pressman; who was anxious simply to bring before them
certain facts, and they could work out their own explanation, possibly
a better one than his. He summoned, as it were, three witnesses. The
first was Mr Britton Harney, a Melbourne journalist, who, within a short
time of the Titanic disaster, received a message, signed W T Stead. The
second was Mrs Charles Bright, well-known in Sydney and Melbourne,
who had been in correspondence with Mr Stead for twenty years, and
had received messages by automatic writing since that gentleman's
passing onward.

An analytical comparison of these independently received
communications gave the impression that they were from the same
individual intelligence, and were quite characteristic of Stead himself.
But there was the addition testimony of Dr James Coates, a cultural
student of psychical phenomena, living at Rothesay, in the West of
Scotland. In his circle Dr Coates had striking evidence of the presence
of the impetuous and enthusiastic journalist, whose presence was
announced in a purely Steadesque manner. All this testimony, with the
additional evidence of the daughter, Miss Estelle Stead, seemed to justify
those who understood these matters in believing that the messages
were genuine.

Several personal experiences were related . . . but the only one of
general interest was that which concerned the late Mr W T Stead.
According to his daughter, she is in frequent communication with her
father, generally by the aid of a spirit-friend, who is described as 'the
little poet'. Miss Stead says that on a recent occasion her 'little poet'
spirit-friend sat writing at night in her room, apparently oblivious to its
earthly occupant. The odd thing was that he could open the door, and
her father, since his transition, had also been able to open it, 'having
been taught to do so by Gordon Knight, the little poet.'

This was followed by another report in June 1914, titled 'Talks with
Mr Stead. Sir A Turner's Psychic Experiences':

General Sir Alfred Turner's psychic experiences, which he related to the
London Spiritualists Alliance in the salon of the Royal Society of British
Artists, cover a very wide field, and they date from his early boyhood.

The most interesting and suggestive relate to the appearance of Mr Stead. On the Sunday following the sinking of the Titanic, Sir Alfred was visiting a medium, when she told him that on the glass on the picture behind his back the head of a man and afterwards his whole form appeared. She described him minutely and said he was holding a child by the hand. He had no doubt that it was Mr Stead, and he wrote immediately to Miss Harper, Mr Stead's private secretary. She replied, saying that on the same day she had seen a similar apparition, and in it Mr Stead was holding a child by the hand.

A few days afterwards (continued Sir Alfred) at a private séance, the voice of Stead came almost immediately and spoke at length. He told them what had happened in the last minutes of the wreck. All those who were on board when the vessel sank soon passed over, but they had not the slightest notion that they were dead. Stead knew, however, and he set to work to try and tell these poor people that they had passed over, and that there was at any rate no more physical suffering for them. Shortly afterwards he was joined by other spirits who took part in the missionary work.

Mr Stead was asked to show himself to the circle. He said, 'Not now, but at Cambridge House.'

At the meeting which took place there, not everybody was sympathetic and the results were poor, except Mr Stead came to them in short, sharp flashes, dressed exactly as he was when on earth.

Since then, said Sir Alfred, he had seen and conversed with Mr Stead many times. When he had shown himself he had said very little, when he did not appear he said a great deal. On the occasion of his last appearance, he said, 'I cannot speak to you. But pursue the truth. Pursue the truth. It is all true.'

I am confident, Sir Alfred declared, that Mr Stead will be the greatest of help to those of us who on Earth worked with him, and to others who believe.

***

William Thomas Stead was born on 5 July 1849, in the Old Manse of the Presbyterian Church in the village of Embleton near Alnwick in Northumberland. He was the second child, and eldest of six sons in the family of nine children born between 1847 and 1863, to the Reverend William Stead (1814–84), to whom he was devoted, and his wife, Isabella (formerly Jobson, 1824–75), a daughter of a Yorkshire farmer. After about a year the family moved to Howdon-on-Tyne near Wallsend, Tyne-and-Wear, where he was home-tutored by his father, who taught him Latin as a second language, and finished his education at Silcoates School in Wakefield, an establishment for the sons of congregational ministers.

In about 1870 he began to write for the Darlington *Northern Echo*, becoming the editor in 1871. He supported Josephine Butler's campaign against the contagious diseases act.

On 10 June 1873, he married Emma Lucy Wilson (1849–1932), at Tynemouth in Northumberland, and they had four sons and two daughters born between 1874 and 1889. His daughter, Estelle, also became interested in spiritualism, and in 1913 she published *My Father: Spiritual and Personal Reminiscences*, in which she stated: 'My father had blue eyes and rugged features of the North, quite a Viking type.'

William left the *Northern Echo* to assist John Morley at the *Pall Mall Gazette*, where he took over as editor, and wrote several influential articles. In 1890 he resigned the editorship of the *Pall Mall Gazette* and co-founded *Review of Reviews*. In 1891 and 1892 he published a number of ghost stories. In 1893 he founded *Borderland*, a spiritual quarterly, and in the same year he visited the Chicago World's Fair. In 1904 he founded the *Daily Paper*, which collapsed after a few weeks. He narrowly avoided bankruptcy and suffered a nervous breakdown. He lived at 5 Smith Square in Westminster from 1904 until his death.

Estelle noted that from Queenstown he wrote home, 'Something is awaiting me (in America), some important work the nature of which will he disclosed in good time. 'But what it is, whether journalistic, spiritual, social, or political, I know not. I await my marching orders, being assured that he who has called me will make clear his good will and pleasure in due season.'

There is a memorial dedicated to him on Fifth Avenue near Central Park in New York, and one situated on Victoria Embankment in London, reads: 'This memorial to a journalist of wide renown was erected near the spot where he worked for more than thirty years by journalists of many lands in recognition of his brilliant gifts, fervent spirit and untiring devotion to the service of his fellow men.'

His younger brother, Francis Herbert, known as F H Stead (1857–1928), was a congregational minister and social reformer, noted for his involvement of the establishment of Browning Hall in Walworth, London, in 1895, which was a social settlement with the aim of trying to get the rich and poor to live more closely together, and he was instrumental in the campaign that led to the Old Age Pension Act of 1908.

Stead made a number of highly informative communications with Estelle and a friend named Pardoe Woodman, and these accurate descriptions of life beyond the veil have been mirrored by thousands of similar communications from other people since. In this, one of several communications, published under the title of *The Blue Island*, Stead said:

> I was at once amazed and delighted, to find so much truth in all I had learnt, for although I believed implicitly, I was not entirely without misgivings upon many minor details.
>
> On my actual passing from earth to spirit life I do not wish to write more than a few lines. From the time my physical life was ended, there was no longer any sense of struggling with overwhelming odds. My first surprise came when (to your understanding I was then dead) I found myself in a position to help people. From being in dire straits myself, to being able to lend a hand to others, was a sudden transition that I was frankly and blankly surprised.
>
> I was also surprised to find a number of friends with me; people I knew had passed over years before. That was the first cause of my realising the change had taken place. I knew it suddenly and was a trifle alarmed. Practically instantaneously I found myself looking; for myself. Just a moment of agitation, momentary only, and then the full and glorious realisation that all I had learned was true. Oh, how badly I needed a telephone at that moment! I felt I could give the papers some headlines for that evening. That was my first realisation; then came helplessness – a reaction – a thought of all my own at home – they didn't know yet. What would they think of me? Here was I, with my telephone out of working order for the present. I was still so near the earth that I could see everything going on there. Where I was I could see the wrecked ship, the people, the whole scene; and that seemed to pull me into action – I could help! And so, in a few seconds I found myself changed from the helpless state to one of action; I was helpful, too, I think.
>
> I pass a little now. The end came and it was all finished with. It was like waiting for a liner to sail; we waited until we were all aboard. I mean we waited until the disaster was complete. The saved – saved; the dead – alive. Then in one whole we moved our scene. It was a strange method of travelling for us all, and we were a strange crew, bound for we knew not where. The whole scene was indescribably pathetic. Many, knowing what had occurred, were in agony of doubt as to their people left behind, and as to their own future state. What would it hold for them? Would they be taken to see Him? What would their sentence be? Others were almost mental wrecks. They knew nothing, they seemed to be uninterested in anything, and their minds were paralysed. A strange crew, indeed, of human souls waiting their ratings in the new land.
>
> A matter of a few minutes in time only, and here were hundreds of bodies floating in the water – dead – hundreds of souls carried through

the air, alive; very much alive, some were. Many realising their death had come, were enraged at their own powerlessness to save their valuables. They fought to save what they had on earth prized so much.

The scene on the boat at the time of striking was not pleasant, but it was as nothing to the scene among the poor souls newly thrust out of their bodies, all unwillingly, it was both heartbreaking and repellent. And thus we waited – waited until all were collected, until all was ready, and then we moved our scene to a different land.

It was a curious journey that; far more stranger than anything I had anticipated. We seemed to rise vertically in the air at terrific speed. As a whole we moved, as if we were on a very large platform, and this was hurled into the air with gigantic strength and speed – yet there was no feeling of in security – we were quite steady. I cannot tell how long our journey lasted, nor how far from the earth we were when we arrived, but it was a gloriously beautiful arrival. It was like walking from an English winter gloom into the radiance of an Indian sky.

There, all was brightness and beauty. We saw this land far off when we were approaching, and those of us who could understand, realised that we were being taken to the place destined for all those people who pass over suddenly – on account of its general appeal. It helps the nerve-racked newcomer to fall into line and regain mental balance very quickly. We arrived feeling, in a sense, proud of ourselves. It was all lightness, brightness. Everything as physical and quite as material in every way as the world we had just finished with.

On arrival we were greeted by welcomes from many old friends and relations who had been dear to each one of us in our earth life. And having arrived, we people who had come over from that ill-fated ship parted company. We were free agents again, though each one of us was in the company of some personal friend who had been over here a long while.

***

During the séance in which Madame de Meissner says she spoke with Major Butt, she also stated that she 'has received word from Rosalie Straus the wife of Isidor Straus, who, she says, dilates on the happiness of her new existence, and the opportunity for doing service for those about her on the fearful night when *Titanic* went down.'

A newspaper article of 1 June 1912 was headlined 'Millionaire's Wife Who Would Not Be Saved':

Mr and Mrs Isidor Straus drowned together, Mrs Straus refusing to leave her husband's side. According to the descriptions given by fellow-passengers, the noted New York millionaire and his wife went to their death together, standing arm in arm on the first cabin deck of the Titanic, Mr Straus quietly and tenderly reassuring his wife so far as he could. As the lifeboats were receding from the scene of the disaster the couple were observed standing still calmly awaiting their inevitable fate.

One passenger, Mr [Charles] Stengel, who related the touching circumstances tonight, said, 'I can never forget Mr and Mrs Straus, who have been Derby and Joan in life, and who were not separated by death. The sailors of the Titanic, in their endeavours to save Mrs Straus, tried to wrench her away from her husband, but she refused to leave his side. Finally the sailors had to abandon their task. Then the boat began to sink, and as the life boats drew away from her we could see the pair standing together arm in arm, Mr Straus bending towards his wife.'

***

It is interesting to gain the scientific view of the life after death theory, and who better to provide it than one of the most famous men of the scientific world, Thomas Edison (1847–1931), who was interviewed by Shaw Desmond for the *Windsor Magazine* in September 1922 in an article titled 'Edison's Spiritualistic Telephone – The Great Inventor's Views of Life after Death' in which he was strangely described as the 'American magician':

'The thing which first struck me,' said Mr Edison, 'was the absurdity of expecting "spirits" to waste their time operating such cumbrous, unscientific media as tables, chairs, and Ouija board with its letters. My convinced belief is merely that if ever the question of life after death, or psychic phenomena generally, is to be solved, it will have to be put on a scientific basis, as chemistry is put, and withdrawn from the hands of the charlatan and the "medium."

'My business has been, and is, to give the scientific investigator or, for that matter, the unscientific – an apparatus which, like the compass of the seaman, will put their investigations upon a scientific basis. This apparatus may perhaps most readily be described as a sort of valve. In exactly the same way as a megaphone increases many times the volume and carrying power of the human voice, so with my "valve" whatever original force is used upon it is increased enormously for purposes of registration the phenomena behind it. It is exactly on the lines of the tiny "valve" which in a modern "powerhouse" can be operated by the finger of a man and so release a hundred thousand horse power.

'Now, I don't make any claims whatever, to prove that the human personality survives what we call "death". All I claim is that any effort caught by my apparatus will be magnified many times, and it does not matter how slight is the effort, it will be sufficient to record whatever there is to be recorded.

'This will settle once and for all the claims of modern physic investigations like Sir Arthur Conan Doyle and others to leave definitely effected communication with the world beyond the grave.

'Frankly; I do not accept the present theories about life and death. I believe, rightly or wrongly, that life is indestructible, it is true, and I also believe that there has always been a fixed quantity of life on this planet, and that this quantity can neither be increased or decreased. But that does not mean that I believe the survival of personality has been proved – as yet. Perhaps it may be one day. Perhaps some apparatus upon the lines of my "valve" may prove it, but that day is not yet. Nor have I as yet secured any results to definitely prove such survival.

'When I wrote my original article upon my apparatus, and the object for which it was made, there went out to the world the entirely inaccurate idea that I had invented a "spirit-finder." The fact is that it is almost impossible to get people to understand, however plainly you put anything.

'Then what is your conception of life, Mr Edison.' I asked.

'What I believe is that our bodies are made up of myriads of units of life. Our body is not itself the unit of life or a unit of life. It is the tiny entities which may be the cells that are the units of life. Let me give you as an example, the famous flier, the steamship Mauretania. The Mauretania is not herself a living thing it is the men in her that are alive. If she is wrecked on the coast, for instance, the men get out and when the men get out it simply means that the life-units leave the ship, but they are not dead yet. And so in the same way a man is not "dead" because his body is buried – and the vital principle – that is, the "life-units" has left the body.

'Everything that pertains to life is still living, and cannot be destroyed. Everything that pertains to life is still subject to the laws of animal life. We still have myriads of cells, and it is the inhabitants of these cells, inhabitants which themselves are beyond the limits of the microscope, which vitalise and run our body.

The point is that the men who were in the Mauretania still live, but they don't live in the Mauretania.

'To put it in another way, I believe that these life-units of which I have spoken band themselves together in order to make a man. We have too facilely assumed that each one of us is himself a unit, just as we have assumed that the horse or dog is each a unit of life. This, I am convinced, is wrong thinking. The fact is that these 'life-units are too tiny to be seen even by the most high-powered microscope, and so we have assumed that the unit is the man which we can see; and have ignored the existence of the real life-units, which are those we cannot see.'

I ventured here to ask how it was that such infinitesimal entities could carry on the tremendous and varied work of, for example, the human body.

'There is nothing to prevent it,' said the great inventor, with assuredness, 'for I have had the calculations made, and the theory of the electron is, in ray view, satisfactory and makes it quite possible to have a highly organised and developed entity like the human body made up of myriads of electrons, themselves invisible.

'Further. I believe that these "life-units" themselves possess memory. If a man burns his hand, the skin will grow in exactly the same pattern again, and with the same lines as the hand originally had before the accident. Now, it would be quite impossible for those hundreds of fine lines to be meticulously reproduced if there were no memory for details behind the rebuilding of them. The skin does not grow that way and in exactly the same pattern again "by chance." There is no chance.'

'But are all these life-units, or entities possessed of the same memory, or are some, so to speak, the builders' labourers, and are others the units which direct those labourers.

'It may be that the great mass of them are workers and a tiny minority directors of the work. That is not a matter about which we can speak with any certainty.

'But what one can say with, some assurance is that these entities cannot be destroyed, and that there are a fixed number of them. They may assemble and reassemble in a thousand different forms from a starfish to a man, but they are the same entitles.

'No man today can set the line as to where "life" begins and ends. Even in the formation of crystals we see a definite ordered plan at work. Certain solutions will always form a particular kind of crystal, without variation. It is not impossible that these life-entities are at work in the mineral and plant, as in what we call the "animal" world.

The question I then put to Edison was. What, in his view, are the supreme problems in connection with these entities and the problem of life after death?

'The thing that really matters is what happens to what one may call the "master" entities – those that direct the others. Eighty-two remarkable operations upon the brain have definitely proved that the seat of our personality lies in that part of the brain known as the fold of Broca. It is not unreasonable to suppose that these entities which direct reside within this fold. The supreme problem is what becomes of these master entities after what we call death, when they leave the body.

'The point is whether these directing entities remain together after the death of the body in which they have been residing, or whether they go about the Universe after breaking up. If they break up and no longer remain as an ensemble, then it looks to me that our personality does not survive death – that is, we do not survive death as individuals.'

94

The final question I put to Mr Edison was: 'Then, if these life-units or entities break up, as you suggest, what becomes of the theory of eternal life?

'If they do break up and do not remain together after the death of the body, then that would mean that the eternal life which so many of us earnestly desire would not be the eternal life and persistence of the individual, as individual, but would be an impersonal eternal life for whatever happens to the life-units, or whatever forms, they may assume, it is at least assured that they themselves live forever. I do hope that personality survives and that we persist. If we do persist upon the other side of the grave, then my apparatus, with its extraordinary delicacy, should one day give us the proof of that persistence, and so of our own eternal life.'

The great Edison has, we all hope, many years of life before him, in which to accomplish his latest, and what to many will seem his most vital task, the solution of the greatest problem in the world; whether man lives forever.

9. END OF THE LINERS

RMS *Carpathia* was built for Cunard by Swan and Hunter at Wallsend in the north-east of England. She was launched on 6 August 1902, and made her maiden voyage on 5 May 1903, sailing from Liverpool to New York City.

Two years after *Carpathia*'s daring rescue mission, the First World War began. It was transformed into a troopship, transporting Canadian and American forces into Europe during the war. On the morning of 17 July 1918, it left Liverpool bound for Boston.

It was struck by three torpedoes from a German U-boat in the Celtic Sea west of Land's End and began to sink. The ship's captain and crew abandoned ship, escaping in lifeboats thanks to the protective force of the nearby HMS *Snowdrop*.

Newspapers reported:

The Carpathia was outward bound. She was torpedoed three times on Wednesday off the Irish coast and sank quickly. The only casualties were five firemen, who are believed to have been killed by the explosion. There were over 200 people on board, including fifty-seven passengers.

The first torpedo struck forward at nine o'clock. The passengers had just finished breakfast. The second torpedo came two minutes later. It exploded in the engine room. The third struck the gunners room. A huge explosion followed. Those on board could see the submarine, which was a big two-masted vessel of the latest type. The first two explosions caused an inrush of water, but the vessel would probably have floated for hours. The third torpedo, however, caused the Carpathia to rapidly settle down.

The first torpedo damaged the wireless and made it impossible to send out a call for help. There was no panic. The officers skilfully handled the situation, and the passengers and crew were in the boats within fifteen minutes. Warships picked up the survivors at midday. The sailors say that the submarine trained her gun upon the boats, and it is certain that she would have opened fire on them but for the arrival of a minesweeper. The third engineer and boiler-master, although badly scalded, gallantly stood by the engines long enough to bring the vessel to a standstill, thus enabling the lifeboats to be launched without delay.

The *Town and Country Journal* in Sydney reported on 3 June 1914 under the headline 'Top of Form RMS *Britannic*':

There was launched at Belfast on February 26 last the White Star triple screw steamer Britannic. The RMS Britannic has a tonnage of 50,000 tons gross register, and will be employed in the Atlantic mail and passenger service of the company. From Messrs Dalgety and Company, Limited, Sydney, who is the Australian agents for the White Star line, we have received a copy of an interesting illustrated booklet, giving a description of the Britannic, the pictures showing the huge leviathan in course of construction. The vessel has a length of 900ft, and in general features is similar to the RMS Olympic. The progress made by the company is shown by a picture of the first Britannic built in 1874, which was 455ft long, and 5004 tons register, and the new Britannic, about 900ft long, and 50,000 tons gross register, now being built.

Under the headline 'Hospital Ship Britannic Sunk' London newspapers reported on 22 November 1916:

The Admiralty reports the hospital ship Britannic, which is the new White Star liner of 48,000 tons, was sunk by a mine or torpedo on the 21st in the Aegean Sea. There are 1106 survivors, 28 of whom were injured. It is estimated 50 were lost.

The Britannic was the fourth largest vessel in the world, being beaten by the Bismarck, 56,000 tons; Vaferland, 54,282 tons; and Imperator. The Olympic, which was fifth on the list, was of 46,369 tons.

London, November 23:

The Chronicle's Athens correspondent says the Britannic was submarined off the Island of Zea. The survivors and nurses were landed at Phaleron and witnessed the departure of two expelled ministers going to the Piraeus.

Details of the outrage prove the Britannic was the victim of another of Germany's unmitigated barbarisms. Two Hun submarines lay in wait in the narrow seas, for the express purpose of sending her to the bottom. The submarines attacked on both sides simultaneously. Each launched a torpedo. One missed, but the other struck the vessel fatally. The deliberate act was all the worse because the submarine commanders must have noticed the Britannic going north, this fact implying she was carrying the usual crew, a complement of nurses, doctors and medical servicemen. They did not count with the cowardly enemy, for the Britannic was going to Mudros to take aboard sick and wounded whereof she was fitted up to carry 3000.

A survivor says that perfect order prevailed. The nurses, like the officers and men of the medical corps, lined up on deck. There was not the slightest suspicion of panic. A stewardess, who was aboard the Titanic when the latter went down, tells a terrible story of the launching of the first two boats near the stern, the ship heeling over and the screw, out of the water, whirling round. Two of the loaded boats were sucked towards it and cut up like matchwood. Many were killed outright and others received horrible wounds.

'Oh!' she exclaimed, 'it was really worse than the Titanic.'

The Britannic was the largest tonnage British vessel afloat, although the Aquitania is longer. She had an extraordinary series of life saving devices, including 48 lifeboats, mostly of 34 feet, some with engines, arranged in tiers across the deck instead of along the bulwarks. Passengers are marshalled on deck in the event of disaster, and take their place before the lifeboats, which are swung out by cranes until clear of the ship. It is also possible to launch the boats on an even keel. Even if the Britannic had listed, six of the main watertight compartments could have been flooded without affecting the safety. In consequence of the Titanic disaster, the Britannic was provided with an inner hull.

The Britannic was torpedoed at 3 o'clock in the morning and sank near the shore 55 minutes later. There were no wounded on board. The ship's complement included 120 nurses and 390 officers and men of the A.M.C.

The islanders of Zea witnessed the sinking of the vessel and the struggle of the victims amid the waves. The women tore off their clothing to make bandages for the injured. Two boats were caught in the propellers and 25 were injured. They are now in the Russian hospital. Others are aboard Allied warships, which quickly dashed out from the Piraeus. A number of mines have been found adrift in Greek waters. Apparently a submarine has been sowing mines broadcast.

Launceston Examiner, 9 November 1935:

'Last of Three Great Sister Ships – The Olympic Ends Her Illustrious Career' The Cunard-White Star liner Olympic is the last of an unlucky trio, her sisters Titanic and Britannic having been sunk soon after completion. The former struck an iceberg off Newfoundland on May 12 (sic), 1912, and foundered with heavy loss of life, and the other was sunk by torpedo on November 21, 1915, when acting as a hospital ship in the Aegean Sea.

An amusing incident occurred when the new liner left New York for England on her first homeward crossing. A passenger, Mr W A Burpee, left his spectacles in his office and wirelessed for them to be sent on to London. Mr Tommy Sopwith, the aircraft manufacturer and yachtsman, heard of Burpee's plight, flew out to the ship in his plane and endeavoured to drop the glasses on the liner's deck. He missed and they were lost.

The United States Government immediately cited the incident as an example of the uselessness of aircraft for bombing warships in time of war. It was stated that if an experienced airman like Mr Sopwith could not drop a case of spectacles on to the deck of the world's largest liner, it would be almost impossible for a 'plane to drop a bomb on a warship steering a zigzag course at over 20 knots. The Olympic soon started her chequered career in earnest. She collided with and nearly sank the British cruiser Hawke in a fog, many lives being lost. The subsequent enquiry lasted months and ended in both ships being found at fault, with the Olympic the more negligent of the two.

Following on the Titanic disaster there was a big drop in the passenger bookings by the Olympic, it being considered that she had insufficient life boat accommodation. Alterations had to be made to regain patronage.

The Olympic's first useful work during the war was to assist in rescuing survivors of the 25,000 ton warship Tenacious, which was mined off the west coast of Ireland. Seven months after the naval authorities converted the mammoth liner into an armed troopship. One 12 pounder and one 4.7 inch gun were set on the poop and the luxurious dining saloon was used as a troop deck. Her first voyage in this connection was to the Dardanelles with 6000 troops.

Flying the White Ensign, armed and fully camouflaged, the Olympic sailed for Murdos (in the Aegean Sea) under the command of Captain Sir Bertram Hayes. She was stopped by destroyers and examined off Gibraltar and Malta, and in the East Mediterranean picked up six men in a lifeboat. They were the survivors from the French steamer Provincia, which had been sunk earlier in the day by a submarine. A few hours later the lookout man sighted a submarine steaming slowly on the surface. An attempt at ramming was unsuccessful, and the 'sub' sent a torpedo after the Olympic. A quick turn saved the ship, and the torpedo passed just behind the rudder of the vessel. May 12, 1918, the sixth anniversary of the sinking of the Titanic, was perhaps one of the most eventful days of her career.

An enemy submarine suddenly appeared a couple of points off the port bow. Evidently its crew was not keeping a look-out and made no attempt to move as the 46,000 ton liner rushed it at over 20 knots and hit it amidships. The two halves floated on the surfaces for a few minutes while terrified men climbed hurriedly out. They were picked up by the American Destroyer, Davis, and both ends were sunk by gunfire. Investigations revealed the sunken submarine to be the U103, which was evidently waiting to torpedo the Olympic, but the liner came up quicker than expected, and the tables were turned.

Sir Bertram Hayes was awarded the D.S.O. and was presented with a handsome cheque from the White Star Line for this feat. As the ship was leaking slowly at the bows she was placed in dry dock for repairs. Curiously enough, parts of another U-boat were found clinging to the rudder, and the propeller blades were chipped. Apparently the Olympic sank two submarines and not one as was at first supposed.

In the latter years of the war enemy submarines hunted in pairs. Lying some distance apart they would allow the intended victim to pass between them, receiving a torpedo from each as she did so. As the Olympic turned to ram the U103, her stern must have struck the second vessel which lay submerged and sunk her with all on board. In the lounge of the Olympic until her last days there hung a tablet with the following inscription: 'This tablet, presented by the 59th Regiment of the United States Infantry, commemorates the sinking of German submarine U103 by the Olympic on the 12th May 1918, in Lat, 49 degrees. 10min. N., Long., 4 degrees. 51min. W.'

In February, 1919, the liner ran up the Red Ensign again, and reclaimed the title of 'RMS', in which guise she carried thousands of Americans back to New York from France and England. The Olympic justly earned the title of 'Old Reliable,' given by all who had served in her. Years later Sir Bertram Hayes, KCMG, DSO, the master of the Olympic during the war and for many years commodore of the White Star Line, referred to her under that name and described her as the finest ship ever built, and the finest that ever would be.

During 1919, while the passenger accommodation was being renovated, engineers converted her engines from coal to oil burning, and she emerged from the yards an almost new ship, being in perfect order and spick and span under a new coat of paint.

For 10 years the 'Old Reliable' ran to schedule in the White Star Line's service between Southampton, Liverpool, and New York, but her age slowly found weak spots and the repair bill grew. Repairers often had charge of her and she became an expensive vessel to run. Four years ago the bed plate beneath the engines became damaged and her sailings for weeks ahead were cancelled. Many thousands of pounds were spent in repairs. About two years ago the vessel crashed into a lightship off the American coast during a thick fog, causing loss of life and heavy damage.

The liner's death knell was rung in 1933 when the Cunard Line and the White Star Line amalgamated. Sailings could not be found for all the combine's vessels, so the older ones were scrapped and the larger ones, which could not be fitted in the schedules, were used as cruising liners.

The former Cunarder, Mauretania, which vessel the Olympic was built to challenge, was painted white and cruised to the Atlantic Islands and the Mediterranean, but the fuel bill was exceptionally high, and she was laid up at Southampton and subsequently sold.

The renowned vessel, which rendered yeoman service to the Empire during the war and after, will be no more. It is the end of the RMS Olympic, alias HMS Olympic, alias – 'Old Reliable' – a sad end after a wonderful career.

Ships come and ships go; some to far distant seas, some to 'Davey Jones's', some to ship-breakers. Built to cater for the enormous cross-ocean trade and the millions of travellers, they eventually grow old and become unprofitable to run. So they are discarded, stripped of all valuables, and scuttled or sold to the highest bidder. It is the way of all ships. That famous 'ocean greyhound,' the Mauretania, which made record crossings of the Atlantic Ocean for 20 years, went to the ship-breakers early this year. Now the largest liner ever completed in a British yard has gone the same way. She is the 45,439 tonner Olympic, which sailed from Southampton last weekend to the ship-breaking yards at Barrow. All ships in the harbour sounded their sirens in salute as she passed.

10. PERSONALITIES

William Thomas Stead

William Thomas Stead was born on 5 July 1849, in the Old Manse of the Presbyterian church in the village of Embleton near Alnwick in Northumberland. He was the second child, and eldest of six sons in the family of nine children born between 1847 and 1863, to the Reverend William Stead (1814–84), to whom he was devoted, and his wife, Isabella (formerly Jobson, 1824–75), a daughter of a Yorkshire farmer. After about a year the family moved to Howdon-on-Tyne near Wallsend, Tyne and Wear, where he was home-tutored by his father, who taught him Latin as a second language, and finished his education at Silcoates School in Wakefield, an establishment for the sons of congregational ministers.

In about 1870 he began to write for the Darlington *Northern Echo*, becoming the editor in 1871. He supported Josephine Butler's campaign against the contagious diseases act.

On 10 June 1873, he married Emma Lucy Wilson (1849–1932), at Tynemouth in Northumberland, and they had four sons and two daughters born between 1874 and 1889.

He left the *Northern Echo* to assist John Morley at the *Pall Mall Gazette*, where he took over as editor, and wrote several influential articles. In 1890 he resigned the editorship of the *Gazette* and co-founded *Review of Reviews*. In 1891 and 1892 he published a number of ghost stories. In 1893 he founded *Borderland*, a spiritual quarterly, and in the same year he visited the Chicago World's Fair. In 1904 he founded the *Daily Paper*, which collapsed after a few weeks. He narrowly avoided bankruptcy and suffered a nervous breakdown. He lived at 5 Smith Square in Westminster from 1904 until his death.

There is a memorial dedicated to him on Fifth Avenue near Central Park in New York; and one situated on Victoria Embankment in London, reads: 'This memorial to a journalist of wide renown was erected near the spot where he worked for more than thirty years by journalists of many lands in recognition of his brilliant gifts, fervent spirit and untiring devotion to the service of his fellow men.'

His younger brother, Francis Herbert, known as F H Stead (1857–1928) was a congregational minister and social reformer, noted for his involvement of the establishment of Browning Hall in Walworth, London, in 1895, which was a social settlement with the aim of trying to get the rich and poor to live more closely together, and he was instrumental in the campaign that led to the Old Age Pension Act of 1908.

In 1913 his daughter, Estelle published *My Father: Spiritual and Personal Reminiscences,* In which she stated:

My father had blue eyes and rugged features of the North, quite a Viking type. His mother belonged to Northumberland. As a boy he was fond of birds and painted them. The story that in Northern Echo days he used to ride into Darlington on a donkey is not quite true – it was a pony.

He read the *Spectator* to us on Sunday afternoons, ending up with the Bank Rate! My mother followed with stories. To ensure that we had been listening, each of us in turn had to fix on some name or episode mentioned; also after chapel at our meal we had to do the same, taking the sermon as our subject. It was a game very much in the manner of 'Twenty Questions'. Every morning each child had to bring to the breakfast table an interesting fact chosen out of the morning newspapers.

Father had fluent but ungrammatical German. He saw to it that all his children had a really good knowledge of French and German. He adored children and had a wonderful way with them, as he had with grown-ups. His *Books for the Bairns* were the genuine result of his affection for children.

He was continually bringing people to Cambridge House, our home at Wimbledon, not only to dinner but to stay. There always seemed to be visitors and my mother's life was not easy, for he would telegraph at the last moment – there was no telephone then – that he could not get away from the office, and she would have to entertain strangers, about whom she knew little, to dinner.

Though in many things my father and mother were not sympathetic, there was a strong bond between them, and I remember him saying that he would not have married anyone else. He gave mother a valentine every year.

He was always being pestered and plagued by men and women who appealed to him, for he was most sympathetic and soft-hearted. He gave his money away with goodwill to everybody who asked and seemed deserving.

One of the worst cases was that of a Russian Princess who told him that she had been sent to him by the Tsarina. In all she must have got £15,000 from him on, it appeared, the security of estates that she owned in Russia. The way he parted with his money was so notorious that the time came when mother had to see that he went out with very little in his pockets. My mother undoubtedly had a better flair for character than my father. She died at eighty-two in 1932.

My father was a demon for work. In the early morning, before going to the office, and after dinner at night, he would be writing. He seldom had much time to spare for holidays, but once he went with my mother on a tandem tricycle to the Lake District. Whenever possible, he would retire to our cottage at Hayling Island and plough through masses of arrears.

He was fond of sailing and the coastguards said they always kept a sharp look-out because he was so venturesome. But he never had an accident, whereas my brothers had several, and at times my father had to go to their rescue. He was a strong breast-stroke swimmer, a keen walker and, to the scandal of Wimbledon in the early days when we were small, would make us all run down the hill on the way to chapel. At one time he was very keen on photography and the walls of our cottage at Hayling were adorned with the results. He also liked gardening. He would have left a fine library had he not lent his books to all and sundry. He had the ability, when in good health, to go to sleep at any time.

He was very sensitive and it hurt him that so few of his Pall Mall staff fully sympathized with him. It is well that it should be explained that he was subject to terrible fits of despondency, when he felt that he had not the power to go on. Then he would suddenly recover.

Harmsworth and a brother came to him for ideas before starting the *Daily Mail*. Many people got ideas for their schemes from him for he never minded having his brains picked. His motto, 'The union of all who love in the service of all who suffer', was chosen when he was discussing with Mrs Besant the idea of a Civic Church.

I never remember him giving much time to preparing his speeches. He would think about what he was going to say but seldom make notes. He had such a wonderful memory.

He took to smoking cigars in the P.M.G. days because when interviewing he found that if he smoked with people he could get them to talk more freely. When in South Africa he began smoking a pipe, using Boer tobacco, but as he could never keep it alight, he gave it up.

With regard to The Daily Paper, his idea was, as he wrote in the *Review of Reviews*, 'to band together all the readers in a great cooperative partnership for the achievement of common ends; to make the newspaper itself not merely a nerve centre for the collection and distribution of news but for the inspiration, direction and organization of the moral, social, political and intellectual forces of the whole community.' He particularly wanted to interest the housewife and so he arranged for delivery in mid-morning after the men had gone to work. The *Daily Paper* experiment was a complete failure. After seeing the first number to press he broke down completely. By the loyal support of those around him the paper was kept going for some weeks but it was soon clear that it was impossible to continue. The doctor advised a voyage to South Africa. Nothing seemed to rouse him until we got to Tenerife when he suddenly decided that there was a good reason for the failure. After that he worked hard, reading and dictating in the morning and romping with the children on board in the afternoon.

When in South Africa, Lord Milner would not receive us because of a speech that father made in Cape Town. Rhodes had long been dead and we stayed at Groote Schuur with Dr Jim. We also stayed with Smuts, Botha, ex-President Steyn and Hertzog, and there is no question that the work that my father did helped to make a good settlement.

When I wanted to go on the stage my father took it very badly and sent me to South Africa again, this time to tell stories in connection with the *Books for the Bairns*. When I came back and still persisted he gave way. Up to this time, of course, he had never seen a stage play. Benson said, 'Send her to me and I will put her through it good and strong', so I joined Benson's company.

My father always felt that he got his directions straight from the 'Senior Partner'. He talked about the 'Senior Partner' long before he took up spiritualism. How did he get his directions? No doubt it was something like the way in which the Quakers feel they get a lead. His visit to the Tsar was one of the instances in which he felt that he had a clear lead.

It was well perhaps that my father died when he did. Had he lived he would have been a disappointed and thwarted man. His physique would not have stood the conditions in which he found himself. His head worried him. He felt he could not do as much as he used to do and that he had lost his influence.

His intention, if he had come back from America, was to have written his memoirs, which he was always looking forward to doing. He could have kept in touch with people he could help and might have recognised that he had done his share and could well be quiet. But would he have been willing?

A portrait of my father was offered to the National Portrait Gallery and refused. There is a copy of the Thames Embankment plaque in New York.

When my brother William died in 1907 my father was just going to make over the *Review of Reviews* to him.

Morgan Andrew Robertson

He was born in New York on 30 September 1861, the son of a ship's captain on the Great Lakes. He served in the Merchant Navy from the age of 16 until 1899, during which time he had risen to first mate, and after a spell as a diamond setter in a New York jeweller's shop, he took to writing maritime fiction stories.

He published another story in the year before his death, entitled *Beyond the Spectrum*. It tells of a sneak attack on the United States naval fleet in Hawaii by Japanese ships, which leads to a war between the United States and Japan. The only difference to the attack on Pearl Harbor in 1941 being that attack was carried out by war planes, which were not so prominent in 1914.

Morgan Robertson was found dead in his room at the Alamac Hotel in Atlantic City, on the afternoon of 24 March 1915, aged 53, the cause of death being a heart attack, brought on by an overdose of the sedative paraldehyde, which he had been taking to help him to sleep. He was actually standing up when he was found, leaning against a bureau, on top of which his head was rested.

Cheiro

William John Warner was born on 1 November 1866, in Rathdown, County Dublin (some sources say Bray in County Wicklow). He was the son of William Warner (1841–1901), and his wife, Margaret (formerly Thompson), who had married at Bray on 1 August 1861. He had an older sister named Sarah Elizabeth (born at Bray in 1864). His father was the schoolmaster of the Bray Bridge School in Bray, and his mother was the daughter of William Thompson, a customs clerk. His middle name was taken from his grandfather John, who worked as a gardener for the Le Touche family.

He took the name Count Louis Hamon or Count Leigh de Hamon. While visiting the Bombay region of India (now Mumbai) he became acquainted with the guru Chitpavan Brahmin, and after studying an ancient book concerning hands for two years, he returned to London where he chose the sobriquet 'Cheiro', derived from the word cheiromancy, meaning palmistry, and soon began to make a name for himself as a society palm reader.

Under the title: 'History's Great Stories' the following article was published in the *Brisbane Truth* for 11 January 1953. It is an abridgement of his memoirs, and contains some interesting anecdotes about his life:

On the foggy Atlantic morning of April 12, 1912 *(sic)*, a stocky, white-bearded man scrambled along the tilting decks of the 'unsinkable' liner

Titanic, soon to make her final plunge after ripping open her hull on an iceberg. As the man moved aside to let a woman pass to a lifeboat, he was overheard to say to a companion: 'Looks like that damned Cheiro was right after all.' William Stead, author, reformer, traveller, was paying tribute in his last moments to a strange personality with amazing powers of prophecy, Count Louis Hamon, known the world over as Cheiro, the Hand.

Though he has been dead for 16 years, experts on the occult are still discussing whence Hamon derived his mystic power. He himself maintained it came from a study of palmistry from the days of ancient Egypt. His admirers claimed he had other occult gifts.

There is no doubt that Hamon warned William Stead almost a year in advance that, 'It will be dangerous for you to travel next April, especially by water. It could mean your death.'

Nevertheless, William Stead embarked on that fateful Titanic maiden voyage and the prediction came true. It could, of course, have been attributed to coincidence had not so many other predictions been fulfilled.

Charles Stewart Parnell, the Irish Statesman, laughed when a young man told him a woman would be his downfall. He had not yet become embroiled with Kitty O'Shea.

Oscar Wilde, the great playwright, then at the height of his fame; ran from the room at the prediction that ruin would come between his 41st and 42nd birthdays. It did. He went to gaol.

Hamon told King Edward VII, Kitchener, Rasputin and Mata Hari, the spy, when and in what circumstances they would die. Edward jested that he had been condemned to death. But it came true. Of course, there are many who tried to trick Hamon and called him a charlatan. The enigma remains to this day.

Louis Hamon was born near the Irish town of Waterford, on 1 November 1866, only child of Count William de Hamon, last of an aristocratic French family who had lived in Ireland for centuries. From his father, young Louis inherited a love of poetry, philosophy and the occult. He spent most of his time pouring over treatises on palmistry. He also received his first sound spanking for predicting the future of yokels at the village pub.

Louis' main ambition then was to be a writer, so at 19, backed by a generous allowance from his father, he set out to conquer Fleet Street. He found editors very cagy. 'His writings', they said, 'were too theoretical'.

While 'travelling by train to see a publisher, Louis made his first outstanding prediction. He was reading a German book on palmistry when a handsome, well-dressed man leant across the carriage 'I see you believe in palm-reading,' he said. 'Tell me about myself.' Louis scrutinised the strong hand and foretold a brilliant future. 'But this,' he added, pointing, 'is where your career suddenly fades – at its peak.'

'And what will be my Waterloo?' asked the stranger quizzically.

'A woman,' replied Louis Hamon.

As the train pulled into the terminus the man smiled and said: 'Here is my card. Most of what you have said tallies with my life, but the woman – no. A man with my problems has no time for women.

As the stranger waved goodbye; Louis glanced at the card. It read, 'Charles Stewart Parnell.'

A few years later the great Irish statesman fell – because of his infatuation for Kitty O'Shea, a married woman.

Louis's failure to make the grade as a writer induced him to travel. He went to Rome, where he delved into ancient books on palmistry in the Vatican library. In Cairo he studied the history of palmistry right back to the Pharaohs.

But it was in mystic India that he found the knowledge he sought. For four months he lived with a sect of Brahmins whose predecessors had evolved a study called Samudriak, or the meaning of the lines of the body, and from that, Kastirika, the science of the lines of the hand.

Dressed in a thin cotton gown and eating goats flesh and rice, Louis lived in a mud hut reading their records day and night. One ancient manuscript was of parchment bound in human skin. The red writing, though centuries old, was as fresh and vivid as when first written.

Louis Hamon was 23 when he returned to London determined to become the greatest palmist of modern times.

He adopted the nom-de-plume 'Cheiro' (pronounced Cairo), derived from Greek meaning hand, and set up a consulting room in Bond Street.

Clients were few until he helped the police solve the murder of a Cockney labourer in the East End. The only clue was a blood-stained hand mark on the door of the room where the man had been killed. Cheiro examined the mark and told the police the crime could have been committed only by a relative. Detectives were inclined to scoff, but when they questioned the relatives, one, previously considered above suspicion, panicked and confessed. In the subsequent publicity Cheiro was made.

The first big wave of clients included the young Australian singer, Nellie Melba, who had just reached London. Cheiro told her she would have both good fortune and bad. In her debut, in 'Lucia di Lammermoor' at Covent Garden, Melba had a triumphant success but the same night a young Russian singer she had befriended, slipped into her hotel, stole £5,000 worth of her jewels, and escaped to the Continent.

One morning in July 1891, an elderly man with shrewd eyes and thin lips, who refused to give his name, came to Cheiro and demanded to know his future. Cheiro was reluctant, but the man persisted. Eventually Cheiro told him, 'Three years from now you will attain the highest position open to you in your profession.'

The man left still not revealing his identity. On 19 July 1894, a messenger arrived at Cheiro's office and demanded his presence at the Courts of Justice. Cheiro was left alone in a gloomy room for some minutes. Then a man entered dressed to the robes of Lord Chief Justice. In Lord Charles Russell, who had just been elevated to the highest position on the Bench, Cheiro recognised his mystery client of three years before.

One night at a party Cheiro was asked to read the hands of some of the guests. One insisted on sitting unseen behind a curtain in which two slits were cut. Through these he thrust a pair of podgy hands. Cheiro was astonished at the degree of brilliance and success shown in the left hand. On the right hand was inscribed the same story – until at a certain point the lines broke and there were signs of ruin. The man asked when his ruin would come. Cheiro replied 'Between your 41st and 42nd years'.

The other guests chuckled, but the owner of the hands dashed from behind the curtains and hurried from the party. He was Oscar Wilde, whose play 'A Woman of No Importance' had opened that very night. Wilde had just turned 41 when he faced his sensational trial and imprisonment.

With editors besieging him for predictions, Cheiro at last realised his ambition to write. He produced a daily palmistry column, but insisted on bigger assignments, too.

In 1894 he went to China to cover the Sino-Japanese War, and later to Russia to report the Russo-Japanese War for a group of American newspapers. Wherever he went he picked up more data on palmistry.

In 1901, when his father died, Cheiro became Count Hamon. He still preferred, however, to be called 'Cheiro'.

Soon afterwards, while visiting Paris Exhibition, he received a summons from the Shah of Persia, Mozaffar ad-Din, who was staying in the French capital. The wizened little Shah first called Cheiro 'Magician' and demanded to know what the future held. He began to laugh and taunt him, and finally demanded to know what was happening that very moment in Tehran, his capital.

Cheiro concentrated for 10 minutes then told him that at that very hour people were rioting in Tehran because of high food prices.

'You are an impostor,' snapped the Shah. 'What you say is impossible. Go.'

Three days later Cheiro was again summoned by the Shah. Mozaffar ad-Din apologised. Despatches he said, had confirmed that riots were actually raging in Tehran at the very hour that Cheiro had spoken of them. Solemnly he bestowed on the palmist the Order of the Lion and Sun of Persia.

[On 12 August the French anarchist, Francois Saison, made an assassination attempt on the Shah's life, as he was riding on his coach through Paris.]

In 1905, in St Petersburg (now Leningrad), Cheiro met Rasputin, the Mad Monk, evil genius of the Czars. Rasputin was intrigued by Cheiro's claims and asked the palmist to foretell his future.

'You will be menaced by poison, knife and bullet,' said Cheiro, 'but your end will be when the icy waters of the Neva close over you.'

The Mad Monk flew into a rage. 'Rasputin can never die,' he shouted.' 'Neither knife, bullet nor poison can harm him. He is greater than the Czar.'

Eleven years later, after many attempts to assassinate him had failed, Rasputin was poisoned, shot, and, still living, was tossed over the Petrovsky Bridge into the Neva.

In 1907, in Petrograd, Cheiro was kidnapped by a band of revolutionists. At their hideout a distraught mother pleaded with him to save her son, who was due to face a Czarist firing squad three days later. Cheiro used his influence at court to save the boy.

Three years later, while crossing the wild mountains of Georgia with a Cossack Prince, Cheiro was captured by bandits. He and his companion were taken to the gang's headquarters, where they were in some fear of their lives. To their surprise, however, the bandit chief embraced them. He was the lad Cheiro had saved from the firing squad. As a result the two prisoners were escorted safely to Tiflis.

From then Cheiro had an amazing run of successful predictions. King Edward VII spoke jestingly of him as 'the man who condemned me to death at 69.' The prediction had been made when the King was the gay Prince of Wales. Edward was 69 when he died in 1910.

Cheiro told Lord Kitchener that he would lose his life either by water or in stormy conditions in 1916. Because of this, Kitchener learnt to swim – all to no avail.

When in May 1916, the British cruiser Hampshire struck a mine on its way to Russia and sank; Kitchener went down with her.

Before World War 1, Cheiro became friendly with a Madame Zelle, later to be known as Mata Hari, the notorious spy. At their first meeting Cheiro told her: 'The cycle you are now commencing will reach its climax about October, 1917. There it will end in violent death for you.' Cheiro met the lovely adventuress many times after that. Their last meeting was in June, 1917, when Cheiro bumped into her masquerading as an Irish peasant in a Dublin cafe. One morning in October, 1917; Mata Hari died before a French firing squad after being found guilty of espionage.

He was a prolific writer, and published 25 books on his travels and findings. He moved to Hollywood in 1933 to write scenarios for a film studio. Cheiro fell into a depression, and ill-health forced him to have to move to a modest home in South California, where he died of a heart attack on 8 October 1936. His widow, the Countess Lena Hamon, said her 70-year-old husband, who had been a friend and adviser to film actors late in life, and to European aristocracy and royalty in his early career, had predicted his own death to the hour the day before he died. The *Daily Mirror* for 10 October 1936, reported: 'Phantom Flowers at Mystic's Death Bed – Miss Edith Phelan, brisk, efficient English nurse, startled Hollywood with her story of the last moments of Count Louis Hamon, of Wicklow, Ireland, better known as Cheiro, the mystic.'

She said: 'Three times the clock tolled the hour of one. At the last moment the whole house was filled with an overpowering fragrance of flowers. There was none in the room and none outside, yet we all smelled the fragrance.

'I was sitting at the head of the stairs except at the last moment. They were deserted and yet they creaked as though an army of people were coming and going. I cannot deny the evidence of my senses, yet I cannot believe them. I am a registered nurse; I have seen hundreds of people die, and I don't believe in spooks. I came to this house four days before my patient died, and I did not even know his name. When doctors called me about midnight I noticed he was sinking. I told his wife he couldn't last long. They were just asking me how long when the clock struck one – my wrist watch showed 12.15. Twice again, at about ten-minute intervals, the clock struck one.'

The story did not end there. A report in the *Daily Mail* for July 1945, under the heading 'Fortune Teller's Ashes Buried after 9 Years' stated:

'The ashes of Cheiro, world-famous fortune-teller to kings and princes, are at peace after nine years' wandering round the world.

When he died in America in 1936 he exacted a death-bed promise from his wife to bury his ashes with his kindred occult spirit, who was his stepson, John Hartland, and herself on death. The widow travelled the world carrying his ashes in a little metal casket, and only returned to England recently, when she sent the casket to be interred in her son's grave at Meltham Cemetery, near Huddersfield, Yorkshire.

'My son and husband were inseparable because both had psychic powers,' she said. 'Although my son was untrained, he had second sight and could foretell happenings in the next few months in the family circle. He was buried in 1942. A psychic sympathy bound them together, and my husband did not want us separated in death.'

When Cheiro died, three strange things happened – the clock struck one three times, the house was filled with the overpowering fragrance of flowers though there were no flowers in the house, and the stairs creaked heavily, though no one was using them.

Cheiro was born William John Warner, of Bray, Wicklow, Ireland. He could trace his family to the Hamons of Normandy, and so by deed poll changed his name to Count Louis le Warner Hamon. His 63-year-old British-born widow is called Countess Mena Hamon.

Madame Sophie Adelaide de Meissner

Sophie Radford was born at the home of her maternal grandparents in Morristown in County Middlesex, New Jersey, on 17 November 1854, the second daughter of two in the family of seven children to Rear Admiral William Radford (1809–90) of the United States Navy, and Mary Elizabeth 'Minnie' Lovell (1829–1903). Towards the end of the American Civil War the family moved to Washington DC.

She fell from a horse while riding in Rock Creek Park in Washington DC, on 22 February 1877, and fractured her skull, remaining unconscious for several weeks. Among callers to the family was Waldemar de Meissner (1852–96), first secretary of the Russian Litigation, and they married on 22 November 1877, and President Hayes attended the ceremony. They had a son named Alexandre 'Sacha' (1879–99), who was born in Washington DC. He became a cornet with the 44th Regiment of Dragoons in the Russian cavalry, and died of a throat infection.

It is not known for sure when Sophie became interested in spiritualism. In her 1917 book *The Adventure Beautiful*, Lilian Whiting stated: 'She is a woman of purely social life, the life of great embassies and courts, but she has a psychic gift.' She said that she communicated from the other side with W T Stead, Archie Butt and Frank Millet.

Sophie spent the last seven years of her life in the Washington DC Home for Incurables, where forty people attended her 100th birthday party. When she died there on 17 April 1957, she had lived to be 102 years old. She was buried at Oak Hill Cemetery in Washington DC.

Major Archibald Butt

Archibald Willingham DeGraffenreid Clarendon 'Archie' Butt was born in Augusta in Georgia, on 26 September 1865, the third son of four in the family of five children to Joshua Willingham Butt (1828–78) and Pamela Robertson (formerly Boggs, 1839–1908). He was educated at the University of the South at Sewanee in Tennessee, where he was editor of the college newspaper, and graduated in 1888.

He started his career as a reporter and worked as a correspondent for several newspapers until 1896, when he became first secretary and attaché to Major Matt Ransom, the United States ambassador to Mexico City.

On 2 January 1900, following the outbreak of the Spanish-American War, Butt joined the United States Volunteers and was posted to the Philippines as Assistant Quartermaster with the rank of captain. He remained in Manila until July 1903. In 1904 Captain Butt was appointed depot quartermaster at Washington DC and in September 1906 he was transferred in the same capacity to Havana in Cuba.

In June 1908 President Theodore Roosevelt appointed Captain Butt as his military aide-de-camp. As well as acting as his military adviser, Butt was expected to accompany the president on numerous social tours and excursions. When William Taft took over from Roosevelt as President of the United States he asked Butt to stay on as his military aide-de-camp and in March 1911 he was promoted to the rank of major.

At this point his health was failing and in March 1912, on the advice of friends, doctors and the president, Major Butt embarked upon a six-week tour of Europe with his good friend the artist Francis Davis 'Frank' Millet. Butt and Millet visited Naples, Gibraltar and Rome, where he had an audience with Pope Pius X, who gave him a letter to deliver to President Taft.

There was some speculation concerning how close the relationship was between Butt and Millet, and there was gossip that the two men were homosexual. The *New York Times* for 3 March 1912 reported quite distinctly on his dandified dress, 'He wore a bright copper-coloured Norfolk jacket fastened by big ball-shaped buttons of red porcelain, a lavender tie, tall bat-wing collar, trousers of the same material as the coat, a derby hat with broad, flat brim, and patent-leather shoes with white tops. The major had a bunch of lilies in his button-hole.'

Following short stays to Berlin and Paris, Major Butt and Frank Millet arrived in England to visit Archie's brother. At 9am on 10 April 1912 he boarded the boat train from King's Cross station to Southampton, where he embarked on *Titanic* as a first-class passenger. Francis Millet boarded *Titanic* at Cherbourg later that day. Archibald Gracie gave evidence to the United States Senate inquiry stating that after the ship struck the iceberg, he saw both Butt and Millet in the smoking room in the company of two other men. They were playing cards and making no attempt to save themselves.

Major Butt and Frank Millet died in the sinking. Millet's body was recovered, but Major Butt's was never identified. The Butt-Millet Memorial Fountain was erected in Washington DC in 1913 to commemorate their names.

Lawrence Beesley

Lawrence Beesley was born at Steeple Grange in Wirksworth, a village in the Peak District of Derbyshire, on New Year's Eve, 31 December 1877. He was the third son of seven in the family of eight children to Henry Beesley (1845–1906), a bank manager, and his wife Anna Maria (formerly James, 1846–1926).

Lawrence was educated at Derby School, and after excelling academically he went up to Gonville and Caius College in Cambridge.

The college was named after the family of Lieutenant Gonville Bromhead, who was awarded the Victoria Cross for the defence of Rorke's Drift, the battle made famous in the film *Zulu!*. Other pupils include Doctor Edward Adrian Wilson, who died with Captain Scott in the Antarctic in 1912; Harold Abrahams, who won the 100 metres gold medal at the 1924 *Chariots of Fire* Olympic Games; and Sir Francis Crick, who discovered and developed the structure of DNA, for which he was awarded the Nobel Prize in Physiology and Medicine in 1969. The University is also famous for entering the Football Associations Challenge Cup for the 1880–81 and 1881–82 seasons.

He began his career as a schoolmaster at Wirksworth Grammar School, before moving to Dulwich College as the science master. In 1957 he was still teaching as principal of the Northwood School of Coaching in Middlesex (now Greater London). He became a Christian Science practitioner, and later became the headmaster of Normandale Preparatory School in Bexhill, London.

At Manchester in 1901 he married Gertrude Cecile 'Cissie' Macbeth, with whom he had a son in 1903 named Alec Macbeth Beesley, who married Dorothy 'Dodie' Smith (1896–1990), the author of *The Hundred and One Dalmatians*. Gertrude died in 1906, and in 1919 he married Muriel 'Molly' Greenwood. It was the second marriage for them both and Lawrence had three more sons.

He escaped from Titanic in lifeboat 13, and only a few months after the sinking he wrote a book on his experiences entitled *The Loss of the SS Titanic: Its Story and Its Lessons*. Several newspapers wrote detailed reviews of the book:

> In the face of many highly coloured and hysterical records of the Titanic disaster, the simple, clear narrative of Mr Beesley is convincing and remarkable. It reveals an unusual power of observation and reflection, and a retentiveness of detail which make his story of genuine value. The whole record is complete and absorbing, but it is on points of much discussion, that the observations of a mind as vivid as that of the author are of vital interest.
>
> Mr Beesley was reading in his berth from 11.15 to the time when the vessel struck. He particularly noticed an increased vibration during this period, and assumed that the speed was higher than at any previous time – at all events, in his waking hours. At 11.45 an extra heave of the engines and a more than obvious dancing motion of the mattress, once repeated, aroused his curiosity. This fact is in direct opposition to reports of the crash and jar of the collision. The bilge keels of the Titanic projected 2 ft. for 300 ft. of her length amidships, with the object of lessening the tendency to roll. 'The Titanic struck the berg with a force

of impact of over a million-foot tons; her places were less than an inch thick, and they must have cut through as a knife cuts paper; there would be no need to list; it would have been better if she had listed and thrown us out on the floor for it would have been an indication that her plates were strong enough to offer, at any rate, some resistance to the blow, and we might all have been safe to-day.'

Many reasons have been advanced for the half-empty condition of many of the lifeboats. Mr Beesley mentions the reluctance of passengers to leave the great ship; their belief in her unsinkable construction; the fact that the passengers were kept in ignorance of the extent of the disaster; the refusal of women to leave; the danger of heavily laden boats buckling in the middle; and in the failure of Captain Smith's plan that boats launched half-full should stand by and pick up passengers passed down from the cargo ports.

The writer emphasizes the absence of panic. From the time when passengers were ordered on deck until their arrival in New York on the Carpathia, the attitude of the crowd was impressive. Even isolated instances of excitement were rare. The author maintains that the first, actual realization, of danger came when the Titanic's rockets showed the quiet crowd on deck that help was sought; but many remained unconvinced. The general conformity to the normal in behaviour is accounted for by the quietness of external conditions; the sense of unreality; and, mainly, by the obedience and respect for authority, and the instinct of self-control which are dominant in the Anglo-Saxon race. This correlation on the part of passengers, officers, and crew was simply obedience to duty, and it was innate rather than the product of reasoned judgment.

In many descriptions there have been definite accounts of an explosion at the time of the actual sinking. This idea is not corroborated by Mr Beesley, who maintains that the noise was not like the sudden roar occasioned by an explosion, but was a succession of stupendous sounds which were the result of the engines and machinery coming loose from their bolts and bearings, and falling through the compartments, and dropping down to the bottom (now the bows) of the shop, where they probably fell through the end and sank first, before the ship. Diagrams appended illustrate this idea.

In finely graphic language Mr Beesley describes the sinking as seen from the lifeboat; the horrible and ominous angle shown by the level of the sea against the porthole lights, demonstrating the slow sinking by the head; the gradual disappearance of those lights; then the convulsion and tremendous noise of falling machinery as the ship swung vertically upright; followed by a slight sinking at the stern, and a slow dive through the closing waters.

Mr Beesley devotes some space to the lessons to be learnt from the disaster. Briefly enumerated, they involve the much-discussed matters of insufficient boat accommodation; the iniquity of forcing the speed (the result of public demand); the weakness of the Titanic's construction in the lack of longitudinal bulkheads; and the urgency of construction on the lines of the Great Eastern, whose bulkhead and compartment structure was of the best type yet discovered, although hitherto regarded as too expensive.

Further, the author urges the necessity of enlarging the 'wireless' staff so that no situation similar to the failure of the Californian to catch the Titanic's message on account of a sleeping operator may occur; and he discusses at some length the advisableness of submarine signalling apparatus, the fixing of steamship routes, and a plan by which each passenger and member of the crew has a numbered seat in a lifeboat and practises compulsory boat drill. There is a vital suggestion that, the modern liner having become so large that the strain on the captain to exercise control over the whole ship has reached an impossible limit, there should be an expert officer to supervise the whole management of the boat organization.

The responsibility of the public in the matter of reforms is enforced by the writer: 'Whoever reads the account of the cries that came to us afloat on the sea from those sinking in the ice-cold water must remember that they were addressed to him just as much as to those who heard them, and that the duty of seeing that reforms are carried out devolves on every one who knows that such cries were heard in utter helplessness the night the Titanic sank.'

In 1958 when the film *A Night to Remember* was being filmed Beesley visited the set and attempted to remain on the ship as the sinking scenes were filmed.

Beesley was living at 75 Carew Street in Northwood, Middlesex, when he died of pneumonia at 66 South Park in Lincoln, on Valentine's Day, 14 February 1967, aged 89.

Margaret (Molly) Brown

Margaret Tobin was born in a hospital on 18 July 1867 (her death certificate states 10 July), at Hannibal near the banks of the Mississippi River in Missouri. She was a daughter of Irish immigrants named John Tobin and Johanna Collins, who had both been previously married (her death certificate gives her mother's maiden name as Laura Collins).

Early in 1941 Gene Fowler (1890–1960), the well-known journalist and dramatist, and a fellow native of Denver of Margaret Tobin, wrote an interesting article about her life:

Molly Tobin, who later became 'The Unsinkable Mrs Brown of the Titanic', grew up in a shack in Hannibal, Missouri. At 15, an illiterate tomboy with flaming red pigtails, she ran away from home, travelled by stagecoach to the gold camp at Leadville, Colorado, and went to work as cook and 'potwalloper'. Three weeks after her arrival she met and married John J Brown, called 'Leadville Johnny' by intimates at the Saddle Bock Saloon.

Leadville Johnny was 37 years old, as homely as a hippopotamus, unlettered, open-fisted. In less than two months after his marriage to 15-year-old Molly, Leadville Johnny struck pay dirt. He was offered £100,000 cash for his claim. He took it, in thousand-dollar bills, and rushed home to 'the prettiest gal in camp'.

'I wanted you to have it,' he said. 'But you got to hide it.'

'Where?' asked Molly.

'You figure that out, honey. It's yours. I'm goin' down to celebrate.'

Early next morning he was brought home by two of his intimates, sober enough to make two requests. One was that the 'boys' would not disturb his pretty young wife; the other that they fetch some kindling and start a fire. The boys put him on a bunk, and then made a fire. Molly rousing from deep sleep, sniffed smoke and screamed. She leaped up, scorched her fingers on the stove lids, and delved among the burning sticks, but it was too late. Of all places she had hidden the money in the stove, and now her fortune had gone up the flue. She began to sob. Johnny rallied somewhat. When it penetrated his haze that the money had been burned, he sat up and said:

'Don't you worry a bit, honey, I'll get more. Lots more.'

Fantastic as it may seem, Leadville Johnny went out that very afternoon and located 'The Little Johnny', one of the greatest producers of gold in Colorado history. It is estimated that he took £4,000,000 from this bonanza.

'Nope,' he said to the men who had bought his other property, 'I won't sell this one.'

The meaning of money began to dawn on Molly. The Browns moved 'up the hill'; where mine owners and bankers had mansions. Leadville Johnny went the limit in building a house for his bride. As a climactic touch, he embedded silver dollars, edge to edge, in the cement floors of every room. But Leadville now was not big enough to hold Molly. She had heard of Denver society, of the Kay balls and salons.

'Denver it is, then,' said Johnny.

The Browns built a mansion there. Leadville Johnny contemplated paving it with gold pieces, but was dissuaded. Still, the new mansion was a show place. Molly tried hard to get into Denver society. She hired the largest orchestras, gave the costliest balls, drove the finest horses, but not with snobbery. She often attended, uninvited, the social functions of her neighbours. Indeed, she became such a nuisance as a 'gate crasher' that the ladies decided to crush her.

As part of a cat-like hoax, Molly was solicited to write a dissertation on Denver society. This she did, labouring at a desk inlaid with gold. Her 'article' appeared, word for word, in a magazine, and she was proud of it until the whole of the city's upper crust began heaving with merriment. The new author's misspellings, fantastic verbiage and artless philosophies were there for all to see. At last, conscious of her ignorance, and shamed by her social shortcomings, Molly left town. Johnny said he guessed he'd stay home.

'I never knowed how to spell and never claimed to,' he said, 'and as far as society is concerned, I ain't aimin' that low. Good-bye honey, and don't forget the name of our bank. It's all yours.'

Denver saw nothing of Mrs Brown for nearly eight years. It was a sensation, then, when she returned to the city, gowned in Parisian creations, and accompanied by two French maids; with whom she conversed fluently in their native language. Indeed, during seven and a half years in European capitals, she had become proficient in five languages.

There were other surprises for the home-towners. Molly had made friends with the Divine Sarah Bernhardt, had received stage lessons, and even contemplated playing the Bernhardt role in L'Aiglon. She had received instruction in painting and singing and had appeared with some success in a charity concert in London. The hardest blow to her critics, however, was the fact that celebrities and titled foreigners made the Brown home their headquarters while visiting Denver.

But despite her education in the polite arts, Molly Brown's real nature was manifest at all times. She permitted herself the luxury of forthright speech, and, if in the mood, cursed like a pit boss.

When Leadville Johnny refused to 'gad about' in Europe and elsewhere, they separated. But he never shut her off from his great purse. He still loved her and wanted her to have a good time.

All he desired for himself was privacy and the privilege of sitting with his shoes off in the parlour.

Mrs Brown acquired a seventy-room house and estate near Now York City. She entertained the Astors and other Eastern notables – all of which agonised her Denver scoffers.

In April of 1912, the home town which had refused flatly to receive Molly as a social equal passionately acclaimed her as its very own celebrity. The SS *Titanic* had gone down, and Molly had been its heroine.

Mrs Brown was 31 when she left Liverpool for New York on the Titanic's maiden voyage. Instead of a girlish slimness, she now was ruggedly and generously fleshed. Nevertheless, she still bubbled with vitality. She sang in the ship's concert and was popular with the

119

travelling notables despite her growing eccentricities. She amused some and terrified others with pistol feats, one of which consisted of tossing grapefruits over the rail and puncturing them before they reached the sea.

Although she spent great sums on clothes, she no longer paid attention to how she wore them. When she travelled, comfort was her primary consideration. So, when Molly decided to take a few turns on deck before retiring, she came from her cabin warmly clad in heavy woollies, with bloomers bought in Switzerland, two Jersey petticoats, a plaid cashmere dress, golf stockings, a muff of Russian sables in which she kept her automatic pistol – and over three frost-defying garments she wore a £12,000 chinchilla opera cloak. If anyone was prepared for collision with an iceberg, Mrs Brown was that person.

In the history of the tragedy, her name appears as one who knew no fear. She did much to calm the women and children. She refused to enter a lifeboat until crew members literally had to throw her in. Once in the boat, however, she seized command. There were only five men aboard, and about 20 women and children.

'Start rowing,' she told the men, 'and head the bow into the sea.'

Keeping an eye on the rowers, she began removing her clothes. With her chinchilla coat she covered three small and shivering children. One by one she divested herself of heroic woollens. She 'rationed' her garments to the women who were the oldest or most frail. It was said she presented a fantastic sight in the light of flares, half standing among the terrified passengers, stripped down to her corset, the beloved Swiss bloomers, and the golf stockings.

One of the rowers seemed on the verge of collapse. 'My heart,' he said.

'Damn your heart!' said Mrs Brown. 'Work those oars.'

She herself now took an oar and began to row. She chose a position in the bow, where she could watch her crew. Her pistol was lashed to her waist with a rope. Her hands blistered and began to bleed. She cut strips from her Swiss bloomers and taped her hands. She kept rowing and swearing. At times, when the morale of her passengers was at its lowest, she would sing.

'The damned critics say I can't sing,' she howled. 'Well, just listen to this.'

She sang from various operas – and kept rowing. She told stories. She gave a history of The Little Johnny. She told of the time the £60,000 went up the flue.

'How much is £60,000,' she asked.

'I'll tell you. It's nothing. Some of you people – the guy here with the heart trouble that I'm curing with oars – are rich. I'm rich. What in hell of it? You can't wear the Social Register for water wings, can you?'

When they were picked up at sea, and everyone was praising Mrs Brown, she was asked: 'How did you manage it?'

'Just typical Brown luck,' she replied. 'I'm unsinkable.'

And ever afterward she was known as 'The Unsinkable Mrs Brown.'

After that voyage she went in for thrills. She took world tours and explored far places, always meeting adventure halfway. Once she almost perished in a monsoon in the China seas. At another time she was in a hotel fire in Florida. But the un-sinkable one was un-burnable as well. She rescued four women and three children from that fire.

In France she was given a Legion of Honour ribbon, with the rank of chevalier, in recognition of her charities and her work in establishing a museum for the relics of Sarah Bernhardt.

She now was legally separated from old Leadville Johnny. But still he had not tied the purse strings. Molly could go where she wanted and do what she wanted. It was his way. As for him, he stayed in the parlour with his shoes off, or bent the elbow with old-time pals.

The Little Johnny continued to pour out gold as from a cornucopia. Although her husband was a mine owner, Mrs Brown always took the side of labour, and sent food, clothing and money to the families of strikers.

During the World War she contributed heavily for the welfare of soldiers, and the Allied nations awarded her all the medals it was possible for a civilian woman to receive. She was recipient of personal congratulations and the thanks of kings and princes.

After the war she took another of her world tours. When reporters met her in New York, she said: 'I'm getting to be more of a lady every day. In Honolulu I learned to play the uke'. In Spain I mastered the native dances. In Switzerland I learned how to yodel. Want to hear me?' And she astonished the customs guards by breaking into Alpine melody.

One day old Leadville Johnny died. In keeping with his character he left no will. There was an un-pretty fight now. The Unsinkable Mrs Brown was left floating with little financial ballast. Her eccentricities were cited; her charities construed as loose business affairs. She was awarded the income of £20,000 annually.

'Just to think,' she said with a gay smile, 'that I burned up three times that much in one bonfire.'

Mrs Margaret Tobin Brown died in October 1932. Apoplexy was the cause. She was buried at Hempstead, Long Island, in surroundings that she loved almost as well as she had loved her Colorado hills.

Margaret Brown had been working with actresses when she died of a brain tumour at the Barbizon Hotel in New York City on 26 October 1932, aged 65.

She was the subject of the 1960 Broadway play *The Unsinkable Molly Brown*, which eventually became the 1964 MGM movie of the same name in which she was portrayed by Debbie Reynolds; and she was portrayed by Kathy Bates in James Cameron's 1997 Oscar-winning film *Titanic*.

Benjamin, Esther and Eva Hart

Esther Bloomfield was born on 13 May 1863, at Stockwell in Surrey (now within the borough of Lambeth in Greater London), and was christened on 16 July that year, at St Barnabas C of E church in nearby Kennington, Surrey. Her parents were a gardener named George (born in about 1844 at St Leonards in Gloucestershire), and his wife Esther (formerly Hayes – born at Cranley in Surrey). They married at Slinfold in Sussex on 15 July 1862.

At the time of the 1871 census the family lived at Stockwell Grove in Lambeth, London, and Esther had a little sister named Alice Charlotte, and an infant brother named William Henry. Minnie, Elizabeth Mary and Henry were born later, and a sister named Kate Jane was born in 1865, but she died a year later. The 1881 census names Esther Bloomfield as a housemaid with the family of George Simpson at Herne Hill in Lambeth.

On 28 November 1881 she married a clerk named George Brook, and had several children, but George died in 1890. She married Benjamin Hart in the West Ham district of Essex in the autumn of 1900. A daughter named Eva Miriam was born at Ilford on 31 January 1905. Eva was educated at St Mary's Convent, which later became St Mary's Hare Park at Gidea Park near Romford. In 1912 the family lived at Slinfold House, Whalebone Grove in Chadwell Heath.

Soon after the disaster a local newspaper reported:

Ilford has her part to play in the latest tragedy of the ocean. On April 2nd last, Mr and Mrs Ben Hart were present at the 'Cauliflower' in their honour prior to their departure for Canada. During the evening they were the recipients of a beautiful Illuminated Address which included the following words: 'And may the Almighty Jahovah send you safe voyage and a prosperous career in the land of your adoption.' Mr Hart was a Jew, and the introduction of the word Jahovah into the Address touched him very much. His emotions were easily aroused and he could barely respond with the tears swimming in his eyes. We see from the papers that Mrs Esther Hart and Miss Eva Hart are among the saved, but there is no mention of Mr Hart, and we fear the worst. Had he gone directly to Canada he would have been safely there by now, but he travelled via New York for the purpose of seeing a relative he had not seen for 30 years. Our hearts send out a wireless message of sympathy to the poor lady and child, deprived as we fear so untimely of their protector and probably of all this world's goods that they had with them, for Mr and Mrs Hart had gone out with a few pounds to start afresh in a new world at an age when most people are thinking of retiring from business.

On returning to Britain, Esther and Eva they lived with Esther's parents. They always maintained that *Titanic* had split in half, and this was proven when the ship was located in 1985. Esther died at Romford on 7 September 1928, aged 65.

Eva put her vocal abilities to good use during her life, including becoming a professional singer in Australia, and she organised entertainment for troops during the Second World War. She stated categorically that she had seen the *Californian* much closer to the scene of the disaster than has been accepted. She was awarded an MBE in 1974, and died at Chadwell Heath on Valentine's Day, 14 February 1996, aged 91.

The house where the family lived is now a care home named Hart House, and a public house in Romford was named the Eva Hart in her honour. A letter that Esther and Eva wrote in the library on *Titanic* was sold at auction in 2014.

Jonathan Shepherd

Jonathan Shepherd was born on 31 March 1880 in Whitehaven. He was one of nine children of James Bromley Shepherd, who was an architect and surveyor, and Johanna Elizabeth (formerly Glover). They married at Great Sankey near Warrington, on Christmas Day, 25 December 1866. At the time of the disaster a newspaper reported: 'Some forty years ago the father himself had a miraculous escape from being lost at sea. At that time he was in America and had booked his passage on the City of Boston which left New York for England, and was never heard of again. She foundered in the Atlantic. Providentially, Mr Shepherd changed his plans at the last minute, and did not sail on the vessel. His family were not aware of the true circumstance, and they mourned him as dead for six months.'

The 1881 census records the family living at 12 Lowther Street in Whitehaven, and a decade later they lived at 9 Church Street. They eventually moved to Blackburn, where the 1901 census records them living at 4 Caton Terrace, although James is recorded as living at a different address in Accrington, where he worked as a textile machine fitter. By 1911 the family are recorded as living at 27 London Road in Blackburn.

Jonathan served an apprenticeship with the firm of boilermakers named James Davenport of the Canal Foundry in Blackburn, after which he secured a place as second engineer on a steamer that traded with China and Japan, and he was in those waters during the war in the Far East in 1894–95. The presents he brought home were said to have included a beautiful tea service, a valuable pair of Satsuma vases, and choice Japanese pictures. He worked for Howard and Bullough, a textile machine manufacturers based at the Globe Works in Accrington, and Hadfield's Steelworks of Sheffield, before moving to Liverpool to commence a seagoing career with the W S Kennaugh and Sons shipping company. Jonathan also served on ships owned by James Chambers and Company as part of the Lancashire Shipping Company based in Liverpool. He joined the White Star Line after obtaining his first-class marine engineer's certificate at Liverpool in 1907.

He served first on *Adriatic* and then on *Olympic* when the collision occurred with HMS *Hawke*. On that occasion he showed remarkable presence of mind, for as soon as he heard the crash he realised that something serious had happened and at once closed the watertight doors. As he did so he was up to his knees in water.

Chief Engineer Joseph Bell, a fellow native of Cumberland, selected Jonathan to accompany him on *Titanic*. However, his father stated: 'My lad did not want to go on the *Titanic*. He would rather have stopped on the *Olympic*. But, Mr Bell, when he was promoted to larger vessels belonging to the White Star Company chose my son to go with him every time. It was an honour that we appreciated, but somehow or another in this instance my boy was reluctant to change ships. Still, he felt it to be his duty, and he went.'

His place of residence when he signed on *Titanic* as a junior assistant engineer was as a lodger at 16 Bellevue Terrace in Nicholstown, Southampton.

Having visited his home in Blackburn a few weeks before going to Belfast, the local paper reported that at the time: 'He was not so jolly when he went away, as he seemed to have an idea that something would happen.'

'Mr Shepherd has another son at sea, Joseph, who is with the Bibby Line, and is now on his way home from Rangoon. He (Jonathan) was on duty on the evening of 14 April 1912. After the collision he helped the other engineers rig pumps in boiler room Number 5, but broke his leg when he slipped into a raised access plate. Leading fireman Frederick Barrett and engineer Herbert Harvey helped him to the pump-room. Shortly afterwards the nearby bulkheads was breached and Jonathan was left helpless as the waters rose around him.'

He was described as: 'A fine young fellow. Muscular, and stood six foot without his boots.' His father stated: 'My lad would remain on duty, sink or swim. He would stick to his post to the last.'

Joseph Hyman

Joseph Abraham Hyman was a Russian Jew, born on 15 February 1881, to Samuel Hyman (born in Russia in 1848) and his wife Leah (born in Poland on 15 September 1853). He had a brother named Henry (1880–1957) and a sister named Etta, who became Mrs Rosenberg. He came to Britain as a young man and settled into Manchester's thriving Jewish community. He married his Manchester-born wife, Esther (formerly Levy) at Prestwich in 1902. It would seem that after their marriage they lived in Scotland, where some descendants are living to this day. By the time of the 1911 census their home address was at 45 Stocks Street in Cheetham Hill, Manchester, and they had five children: Julius was born in Glasgow in 1903; Annie was born in Glasgow in 1904; Lilian was born in Kilmarnock in 1906; and Morris was born in Glasgow in 1907. They moved to Manchester in about 1908, where Ena was born in 1909.

Abraham is remembered as a quiet man. He was stated to be aged 34 and was described as a framer living at 34 Lord Street in Cheetham Hill, Manchester, when he boarded the *Titanic* as a third-class passenger going to America to join his brother Harry, who lived at 1369 North Street, Springfield, Massachusetts, with the aim to set up a new life there, and his wife and family were going to join him once he had got established. He left a graphic account of the dreadful events that occurred as the disaster unfolded.

While he was recuperating in New York he noticed how the shops were aimed at the city's cosmopolitan population, and during his stay there he saw a delicatessen that specialised in kosher food and decided to try to establish one when he returned to England. However, he was too scared to get back onto a ship, but his family were still back in Manchester, and after receiving news of the tragedy his wife refused to sail across the Atlantic, so the only way he could summon up the nerve to get back home was after his brother had got him drunk.

When he arrived back in Manchester he set up a small delicatessen at 230 Waterloo Road, Cheetham Hill, modelled on the one he had seen in New York, and named it J A Hyman Limited. Abraham's well-thumbed book containing traditional recipes such as curing salt beef and gefilte fish still exists. Word of his amazing escape from *Titanic* spread around the area, and he became a local celebrity where people would point and say: 'Look it's the man from the Titanic.' It didn't take long for the shop to be known as 'Titanic's', which was incorporated into the name, and is still used by most of the customers of J A Hyman (Titanics) Limited to this day.

He and Esther had two more children, Jonas (born in 1913) and Rachel (born in 1915), and the family lived at the shop on Waterloo

Road. Sadly, Esther died there on 14 September 1927, aged 46. He remarried on 9 June 1929, at the New Kahal Chassidim Synagogue. His new wife was also called Esther, a widow who lived a few doors away at 385 Waterloo Road. She was born at Cheetham in 1886, and her maiden name was Rosengrass. She had married a jeweller named Abraham Libbert in 1909, but he died in 1921. They had a son and daughter named Jack and Fanny; so Joseph was now the head of a family of seven children and two stepchildren.

They moved to Southport, where Esther died on 9 June 1951, aged 65, so Joseph returned to Manchester, where he lived at 25 Crumpsall Lane in Crumpsall. He died at the Victoria Memorial Jewish Hospital on 6 March 1956, aged 75, and he was buried in the North Manchester Jewish Cemetery in Blackley, Manchester.

The Hymans and the families of other victims attended a memorial event in Southampton on 10 April 2012, the centenary of the day *Titanic* left that town to begin its ill-fated journey, and a descendant stated: 'Joseph used to wake up every night screaming with nightmares that lasted for the rest of his life. Then, there were no psychiatrists or recognised conditions such as post-traumatic stress disorder.'

WORLD'S GREATEST SHIPYARD
(From *Freeman's Magazine*, 18 July 1907)

At recurring periods Australians read of another great ship being launched from the yards of Harland Wolff of Belfast. A sketch of the firm, which is the world's greatest shipbuilding concern, should prove of practical interest to Australians who are now entering on a new era of shipbuilding owing to the proposal to construct torpedo vessels in Australian shipyards.

Bram Stoker, who visited the works, writes in *The World's Work*:

Less than fifty years ago the firm of Harland and Wolff was a small, un-ambitious concern. It was only when the manager, Mr – afterwards Sir Edward Harland – acquired possession that expansive power began to manifest itself. It was not; however, until Lord Pirrie took command that full development was reached. For close on forty years he has been connected with the firm, first as partner, latterly as head.

In this shipyard it is possible to follow the whole process of construction, from the reception of the raw material – in itself a big work – to the departure of the registered ship. All day the sound of clattering metal is heard on the stone pavement of the Queen's Road, great wagons are carrying lengths of flat or angle steel. Brass, copper lead, iron, tin, and even costlier metals pass along. There comes also an endless procession of tree trunks – English oak and Irish ash; paint, rubber, cement, canvas, goods for upholstery in every form; and in addition to raw material, anchors and chains, cables and howsers of steel or hemp or coir, ventilators, lamps, and electric and other fittings may be divided broadly into two sections; first, the shipyard proper, where the 'ship' is put together; and, secondly, the different series of stores for raw and completed material, power-houses, workshops, and administration buildings. In the latter section the timber is dealt with in its various stages. There are acres devoted to the preparation of this material alone; ponds for steeping (for certain woods require to be 'seasoned' in various ways), and, sheds for drying both in bulk and in cut form.

Here may be seen fine-grained yellow pine from Canadian slow-growing forests; great teak-balks from Rangoon; enormous trunks, roughly squared by the axe, of giant mahogany from Honduras; hardwoods of beautiful texture and pattern, suitable for panelling and veneering, from Californian mountain woods; from Pacific Islands, from tropical rivers. The odour of the dry, dust of yellow pine and the damp dust of teak blend and give a strange and unique aroma to the place.

The other great building in this section is that devoted to the boiler shops. The main building is no less than six hundred feet long. The boilers for the great ships are of huge size and thickness of steel, fortified by enveloping bands of inch-and-a-half of steel.

In this area of the yard are also the pattern shop, fitting shop, spar and rigger shed sail loft, and boatshed. The newest building in the section is the electric generating station – in itself an example of up-to-date perfection.

The Shipyard Proper is surrounded on three sides by water; to the south the Abercorn Basin, to the north and west the River Lagan. On the south end are five slips – always occupied – and on the north four, and no sooner is a vessel launched than preparations begin for laying the keel of another. Perhaps the most remarkable of many remarkable things is the perfection of the establishment's organisation – no slight matter in an industry where the type of work is constantly changing and where weights and measurements grow by leaps and bounds. At the north end of the yard the space has had to be increased by adding the low-water shore and making it available by shutting out the tide with coffer dams. There are in the yard three enormous travelling gantries, viz., vast bridges supported by trestles, which move on rollers working on firmly laid rails. On these the cranes lift and shift material for the ship beneath.

These gantries cost something like £25,000 each, so that the widening is an elaborate and costly undertaking. Yet at the south end of the yard has lately been erected a still larger, gantry costing perhaps as much as four of the older pattern. The bridge is stationary, 600 feet long, and supported by mammoth uprights. Along this works the travelling double or 'bridge' crane whose top is 185 feet above the ground. It is wide enough to cover two great ships one on each side. By electric power it lifts any weight and deposits it where required. It travels the whole length of the bridge in one minute. It is so arranged that if only one side of the crane is working, or if one is carrying a heavier weight than the other, a supplementary weight travels automatically on the other side so as to keep even balance. In addition to the traveller, this bridge has supplementary cranes, also moveable from which are suspended the hydraulic riveters, which now play so important a part in iron structures. For some purposes the ordinary riveter's hammer is not sufficient, and the by hydraulic riveter is used. It is an immense double mass of steel, shaped like a lobster's claw. When the points are adjusted pressure is applied, and in an instant the great fiery bolt is squeezed into a solid mass inextricably one with the plates it holds.

The first operation in building is, of course, the laying of the keel, already drilled with holes for riveting, to which are bolted the various ribs already prepared. Then along its centre is fixed a single, sheet of steel plating, some four feet high, making one of the divisions between the double bottoms of the ship. From the keel bottom other plating is curved, and this spreading upward and outward fixes the base lines of bow and stern. Amidships the plating is carried out laterally as the ship's bottom is here quite flat.

Close, in front of the ship, lying alongside the sea wall is one of the latest ships launched from the yard, and as yet the largest. She is being 'finished,' and three thousand men are at work on the job. She is the new White Star boat Adriatic, 708 feet long, beam 75 feet, gross tonnage 24,000. Her engines alone weigh 3000 tons, and when her captain stands on the bridge he will be a hundred feet above the keel.

There are at present nine great ships on the stocks in this yard, ranging in length from 400 to 650 feet, with corresponding tonnage of 6000 to 23,000. For many reasons a ship is not nearly complete when she leaves the slip. For the output of a yard is limited by the number of available slips. And even in an incomplete state the weight of a great ship is such as to create an exceeding difficulty of movement. When the Great Eastern was launched there were many unsuccessful attempts before she could be moved; the snapping of a hawser under the terrific strain put on it resulted in a large death-roll. Since that time, however, much has been learned. Now the actual keel does not slide at all; it is the casing under it which slides and this is in a trough of tallow. The mere appearance of these vessels towering over one makes one exclaim, 'Here we undoubtedly find efficiency.'

The very yard is an instance, and no mean one, of human endeavour. Originally a slab formed by the embouchement of a river on a tidal shore, it had in itself but little stability, and was not used for any work of magnitude. It was known as Queen's Island. Then it became a pleasure garden with small zoological annexe. As in its existing capacity it had to be prepared for the reception and sustaining of vast weights, it had to be banked and built up on every side. Embedded in its depths are thousands and thousands of piles, representing an enormous sum of money and an incredible bulk of material. The labour and expense of pile-driving on such a gigantic scale must have been immense. It is such investment of capital – in a whole investment made with forethought and boldness – to which is due the success of great enterprises. Shipbuilding as a venture at the outset must always be expensive.

All through this great shipyard, the biggest and finest and best-established in the world, there is omnipresent, evidence of genius and forethought, of experience and skill, of organisation complete and triumphant. In the doing of this great work – so various, so interdependent – all seems simple, whether it is in perfected details or vast combination. The building of a ship appears to be mere child's play.

Some twelve thousand men are employed here all the year round. At half-past five o'clock on Friday afternoon a horn blows, and section by section the men line up outside the score of pay offices. At twenty minutes to six the last man passes out with his salary. As there are twelve thousand people employed at an average weekly wage bill of £20,000, the payment of these varying accounts within ten minutes instances the perfection of business organisation, which can hardly be exemplified in a better or more fitting manner.

On 1 June 1911, the *Daily Telegraph* reported 'Launch of the Titanic – Successful Ceremony – Two Ships Cost £3,000,000'.

While the Olympic, the first 45,000 tonner in the world's mercantile marine, rode easily at her anchors in Belfast Lough, at noon to-day, the Titanic, her twin sister, of equally heroic proportions, left the ways in Harland and Wolff's yard to join her in a conquering mission in the world's commerce.

The Titanic is the younger sister, although a twin; but in seven or eight months she will be in might, power, magnificence, and usefulness the equal of the Olympic. They will make a colossal pair and will teach the traders of the Old and New Worlds that for enterprise and efficiency British ship owners and British shipbuilders still yield to none.

The many thousands who witnessed the launch will not forget the scene. The Titanic, a gigantic, though an incomplete and ineffective mass, vacated her berth on the stocks with becoming dignity. She was punctual in entering her native element, but declined to be hurried. She did not thunder down the ways to dash upon the muddy bosom of the Lagan, and cause huge waves to sweep up and down the river, and tell the tale that a new monster had been created to plough the seas. On the contrary, the Titanic slipped into the water steadily, magnificently, as if conscious of her enormous bulk and strength, but wishing not to alarm the deep sea monsters with whom she is to be on friendly terms for as long as a modern ship can last. She began to move a few moments after the second of two rockets had told the waiting multitude to be prepared for a great event.

From the time the leviathan commenced her progress towards the water till her bows had plunged 62 seconds elapsed. The Dreadnought cruiser Princess Royal, a few weeks ago, at Barrow, was so impetuous that she became buoyant in well under a minute after the hydraulic rams had started her moving. The Titanic had farther to go, but she appeared much more leisurely than the time of her passage riverward indicated, and she received her baptism while sliding through a bed of tallow at a pace of twelve knots. The warship's ways were much steeper than those of the ship of peace. When the Titanic sat upon the waters she displaced between 24,000 and 25,000 tons – an enormous increase upon the launching weight of the Princess Royal.

Although strength may have a great fascination, the graceful lines and towering sides of the merchantman made the launching of today infinitely more impressive. It was a very great day for Belfast. Here, in the river, were two ships representing a Board of Trade gross tonnage of more than 90,000 tons – the one vessel about to commence her trials, the other taking the water for the first time.

This was not the only reason for the delight of the people who assembled on both banks of the river. The double event was, of course, sufficient to make those who live by the building of ships in Belfast enthusiastic, and the real significance of what the Olympic and Titanic have done for Belfast can be measured by their cost. The wages bill has been enormous, and the cost of materials has meant a great deal to other parts of the kingdom. Combined, the two have made up a bill of £3,000,000 sterling. It may be that this flow of money into the pocket of Belfast was attracted by the guiding hand of the firm of builders of the ships. The genius who designed the Olympic and Titanic and superintended their construction from keel to truck is, I am told by a leading official in the yard, Lord Pirrie. And it so happens that the Olympic leaves Irish waters and the Titanic enters them on the birthdays of both Lord Pirrie and his wife.

Belfast regards this as a day of good omen, and while the whole of the sirens of the ships in the harbour nearly drowned the cheers of delighted thousands today, they could not hide, loud as they were, the sincere congratulations of people who owe so much to the enterprise, initiative, and business capacity of Belfast's greatest captain of industry.

Among those who witnessed the launch besides Lord Pirrie, were Mr J Bruce Ismay, the head of the White Star line; Mr Pierpont Morgan, the head of the International Mercantile Marine; Mr E C Morgan, of Morgan, Grenfell and Company; Mr Charles F Torrey, managing director of the Atlantic Transport line; Mr John Lee, formerly White Star line manager in New York; the Lord Mayor of Belfast, and the Lady Mayoress.

Lord Pirrie superintended the launching arrangements. For hours, great gangs of men used their brawn and muscle to knock away the heavy timbers which shored up the massive hull beneath the fore part of the ship. Where she rested on the ways, were two great arms, like double-bladed propellers. The lower blades were pressed hard by hydraulic levers, and the upper blades rested firmly against the cradles on the port and starboard sides which held the ship upright. By 12 o'clock all the supports had been carried away. A rocket fired high up on the gantry warned the workers that the gauges were registering a pressure which indicated that the Titanic was lively and was ready for launching. The companies of men, with their big-headed hammers, drew up in line on the port and starboard sides, and formed a guard of honour of which the ship, if she had been human, would rightly have been proud. Then a second rocket burst, alarming myriads of sea fowl which circled over the Titanic at the moment when the hydraulic levers were released, and the cradles crashed back the blades of metal which held the vessel in check. Then she moved down into the river. Once in the water the drags and anchors steadied the Titanic, and in a brief time she was ready for the attention of those who are entrusted with the duty of completing her.

Some particulars of the Titanic, in addition to those published in the *Daily Telegraph* today, will be of interest. Her dimensions thus compare with the Cunarder, *Lusitania,* and the fleetest of ocean greyhounds: Mauretania – Tons, 31,938; length between perpendiculars, 762 feet; breadth, 88 feet; depth, 57 feet; speed, 25 knots; built 1907. Titanic – Tons, 45,000; length between perpendiculars. 882 ft.; breadth, 92ft. 6in; depth, 62ft.; speed, 21 knots; built 1911.

The largest beam in the Titanic weighs more than four tons, and measures 92ft. The longest steel plates are 36ft, and there are 2½ million rivets in the ship. The Titanic will have, in addition to dining saloons, lounges, drawing rooms and smoking rooms, several restaurants and veranda cafe. She is to have a splendidly equipped Turkish bath, a swimming bath, and a full-sized racquets court. Passenger accommodation is planned for 750 first-class, 515 second-class, and 1100 third-class, and the crew will number 860.

Appendix II

WHAT THE TITANIC
WAS LIKE

It is interesting to note opinions concerning *Titanic* and other liners of the time from two men who had engineering know-how, and on 18 April 1912, *The Hampton Magazine* in New York published an article entitled *What the Titanic was Like,* by Frank Parker Stockbridge (1870–1940) and Thomas Rutherford MacMechen (1869–1958). Stockbridge was a respected American journalist and author, who was editor of *Popular Mechanics* from 1913 to 1915, and MacMechen was a well-known American aeronautical engineer:

The thousand-foot ship has been a vision in the minds of shipbuilders ever since steam drove the sailing packets from the international highways. When steel replaced iron in naval construction it became theoretically possible. But the transmutation of theory into fact must always, in these commercial days, wait on the test of the touchstone of business. And that touchstone is the simple phrase: 'Will it pay?'

Today, for the first time, engineering science and sound commercial principles give a unanimous 'Yes,' and in a very short time we will see the realization of the dream. There will yet be ships built for speed, and for higher speeds than have been dreamed of by naval engineers, and at some distant day it is conceivable that some of these may reach, the length, of a thousand feet. But that day is not yet in sight, its approach is not indicated by the observable signs of the times, while there are indications that the future ocean greyhound, subsidized for mail carrying in time of peace, and scout service in time of war will tend to smaller than rather larger carrying capacity, for speed at sea is not yet commercially profitable, and it is to the Olympia rather than to the Lusitania and Mauretania that we must look for the prototype of the thousand-foot ship.

Ocean greyhounds like these swift Cunarders cost too much in fuel, too large a proportion of the interior space is occupied by boilers and engines to be carriers of the profitable type. The British Government paid a large part of the cost of their construction and it grants an annual subsidy to their owners as a war measure. The seagoing skyscraper will be built and operated as a commercial venture and so it will be a six-day boat, or, like the new White Star liner Gigantic, even a seven day boat, loafing across the Atlantic in security, and the utmost of comfort, rather than a five-day or four-day racer speeding against time. The floating hotel is already an accomplished fact. Beginning with the President Lincoln and President Grant of the Hamburg-American line, developed in their Cincinnati and Cleveland and the later North German-Lloyd ship George Washington, its present day culmination is found in the White Star Olympic, of which the Titanic was a sister ship. So completely have these ships proved their commercial value that already the keel blocks have been placed for even greater vessels, the Cunarder Aquitania, the Hamburg American Imperator, and the White Star Gigantic. From these it is but a trifling step to the thousand-footer. A description, then, of the ship that will stretch more than a furlong and a half along the fairway is not in the light of what has already been achieved, a difficult picture to draw. It will be a little bigger and a little more comfortable, a little more luxurious than any of its predecessors. But with the increase of luxury at sea there has been a comparative decrease in the cost to the individual passenger, in proportion to what he gets for his money.

So it seems certain that as more and more palatial floating hotels are added to the Atlantic ferry fleet, more and more will the public use them, not merely as a means of travel, but as homes in as true a sense of the word as are the palatial suites of millionaires in the elegant hotels of New York and Chicago.

The nine hundred-foot Imperator, with its 10 stones of decks, is to have scores of private suites, with private dining rooms if desired, all connected by telephones over distances of city blocks, with a Ritz-Carlton restaurant, winter palm garden, children's nursery, conservatory from which the passengers may obtain fresh cut flowers, grill rooms, Roman baths, a swimming pool, tennis courts, gymnasium, and a running track. Many of these features are already included in the equipment of floating hotels already navigating, while the owners of the Gigantic announce a fair-sized cricket field as an added attraction. On the top-most deck of the Olympic and the Titanic was built to similar plans – with a sweeping view of the sea are the most-expensive quarters, costing from £240 to £430 a suite for a single transatlantic voyage. The roomy sleeping-cabins are equipped not with berths but with, brass beds, side by side. The suites contain drawing rooms, dining rooms, and even libraries, to say nothing of luxuriously fitted bathrooms, and all lighted not by portholes but by large, square sash, windows letting in the daylight, by which the passenger can read all that he will ever know of the bygone floating prisons they called passenger ships not many years ago.

The fortunate occupant of one of these suites is surrounded by silken hangings, and costly furniture of mahogany, cherry, copper, and brass. He is warmed by electricity and breathes purified air that flows through ventilators into each room, changed eight to ten times an hour, its temperature being regulated by thermostats and the proper content of humidity given by sprays of steam as the noiseless fans force it into the ventilating tubes. Even in the private bathroom luxury is carried to its limit. Tiled and polished, these rooms are equipped with showers and with such other conveniences as electric curling tong heaters. Electric cigar lighters are provided for smokers, and vacuum cleaners are used to keep all quarters in perfect sanitary condition.

Two other classes of passengers outside of the steerage occupy quietly elegant quarters on the promenade deck and along the awning or sun decks. Even here there is enough Aladdin-like necromancy to teach the traveller, during one voyage, more about utilizing space and filling living rooms artistically than he could learn from a hundred books on housing. Lounges are converted into comfortable single beds, wash stands are hidden within tables, a large wardrobe suddenly becomes a writing desk, or a big mirror is transformed into a serving table. To keep several thousand travellers interested throughout a voyage of from six to 10 days on the huge, slow liner of the present and future, it is the policy that wonders must never cease. Therefore Johan Poppe, designer for the North German-Lloyd Company, devised the plan that has been generally adopted for overcoming the cramped effect of a ship's broken up interior and low ceilings. Saloons and music rooms with vaulted arches of cathedral glass now extend across the entire width of the floating hotels, while richly carved balustrades, splendid paintings, fittings of rare woods, and delicately tinted upholstery add splendour and luxury.

It will be difficult for the thousand-foot ship to provide anything more richly elegant than some of the existing ladies' parlours in the style of the First Empire, with avails of soft reds or blues, matching rugs that yield to the slightest pressure of the foot, and containing beautiful fireplaces and mantels, with many nooks and cosy corners. Nor can the thousand-footer improve, except in the matter of size, on the comfortable libraries in polished oak, and smoking rooms in yellows, greys, and deft blues with crimson leather seats that such ships as the Olympic offer today.

Perhaps the 'family ship' of the future will go farther than those of to-day in provision for the comfort and entertainment of the children, but it will rack the ingenuity of her designer to do so, for the up-to-date seagoing hostelry provides the kiddies with their own. Play rooms and dining rooms, the former, equipped with the best games devised to occupy the juvenile mind, the latter with its long tables and low chairs, looking like a scene in Lilliput land, while the walls of both are gay with scenes from fairy tales.

It was no especial hardship in the old days of the three-decked ship for the passengers to climb the narrow ladder-like companion ways. Today, however, these have given place to broad, ornamental staircases that would grace a palace, and the electric elevator is a regular part of the equipment of the up-to-date liner. Unless the thousand-footer shall replace both stairs and elevator with escalators, it would seem as though the last word had been said in the matter of making the trip from the state room to dining room easy.

For the entertainment of its passengers the modern ship carries its band, usually composed of second-cabin stewards, who are employed as much for their musical ability as for their other qualifications. The daily promenade concert on brass instruments in the morning; the concert by the string orchestra during the dinner hour; and the orchestra concert in the second cabin in the evening, give these musical tars plenty to do to earn their pay. Hops and amateur theatrical entertainments have long been a feature of life on the passenger steamer. The thousand-footer may improve on these forms of entertainment, by providing a roof garden and a troupe of vaudeville performers and taking along a symphony orchestra, but these improvements will be only in quality and not in the nature of an innovation. Nor will it be a novelty for the thousand-foot ship to contain a church, for the Olympic already has a pipe organ in the saloon in which religious services are held, while it is planned that the Imperator shall have a completely equipped chapel.

Instead of the salt meats of 20 years ago, both cabin and steerage passengers have fresh meat daily. Twenty-eight thousand pounds of meat and 15,000 litres of beer were consumed by the passengers of angle North German-Lloyd liner on one recent voyage, while on the same ship the cost of setting the table for a single year was $4,000,000. Sea air whets the appetite when one is idly waiting for the sight of land. Passengers must not only have their regular three meals a day, but might be fed between meals. Light refreshments are served on deck at 10.30 am, and tea at 4 pm. And the end of all this is that 60,000 pieces of soiled linen goes to the laundry to be returned in four days, every time one of the great liners arrives in New York.

Who does not want to take an ocean voyage under these conditions of comfort, not to say luxury? Nearly everybody wants to go to Europe. There is no longer any real obstacle in the way. Have you hesitated because of fear of shipwreck? No storm ever raged that could wreck the thousand-foot ship. Is seasickness the terror of the deep that is keeping you at home? The newest ocean liners have been rendered seasick-proof by rolling tanks which hold the vessel on an even keel in the roughest weather. These tanks, running the width of the ship, are partly tilled with water and are so contrived that they counteract the movement of the waves. The Victoria Line, equipped with these tanks, has reduced the rolling rough weather from 1 degree to less than 2. She recently crossed the Atlantic, encountering severe storms, yet proved so steady that dances were held in the ballroom each evening throughout the voyage.

As the capacity of the ship increases, the cost per ton mile decreases and fares go down accordingly. As against the Imperator's announced capacity of 4,250 passengers without crowding, the thousand-footer will carry 6,000 comfortably – the entire population of a fourth-rate American city – more than the combined capacity of New York's three largest hotels! To the daily life on shipboard, easily pictured from what has already been told of the facilities for rest and pleasure, what has the land to offer that is not available at sea? The passenger arises in the morning from a bed as comfortable as skill can make it, inhales an invigorating breath of salt air, drinks a cup of coffee or chocolate brought to the bedside, slips into the gymnasium for the morning calisthenics, bathes luxuriously either in a private tub or under the shower, with perhaps a plunge in the swimming tank as a final awakener, summons a barber and turns out for a 'constitutional' about the promenade deck before breakfast. Three times around the main deck of the Imperator will measure a mile, and the most jaded appetite responds to the exercise that fills the lungs with clean, dustless ozone.

At the breakfast table he finds the daily newspaper at his plate, still damp from the press, with not only the current gossip of the ship, but the News of the world, flashed by wireless, stock market quotations, and all. Breakfast over, the opportunities for entertainment are almost limitless. One may select a book or magazine from the library, if a reader; play at one's favourite game – provided that it is almost anything but billiards – or indulge one's tastes in practically any manner possible on land. If interested in stocks the passenger can watch market fluctuations reported by wireless throughout the day, and orders to brokers to buy or sell, for that matter, any other kind of business messages, may be sent to any part of the world quite as quickly as though one were on land. Then luncheon, perhaps in the pool, after a morning spent in congenial diversions. Here, on some of the big ships, not only may the gourmet select his chop or steak from the glass-walled refrigerator and see it broiled exactly as he wants it, but he may even pick out a brook trout from many swimming in a tank of fresh water and look on while the chef captures, kills, and cooks it for him! After luncheon there may be a visit to the conservatory to buy a nosegay of fresh cut blossoms or a gardenia for a boutonniere. Perhaps a little kodakiner, and for the amateur photographer there is a dark room, completely equipped for developing and printing negatives. Afternoon tea, served on deck or in the ladies' reception room, breaks the monotony of a motor-less afternoon – for motoring is one sport that cannot be indulged in on ship board – with perhaps another light meal before the formal, evening dress, perfectly served dinner, a concert, a theatrical entertainment, a lecture or a ball fills an evening that brings a joyous, restful day to its close, while a Turkish bath just before turning in prepares the voyager for refreshing sleep. Yet even more interesting in many respects than the wonders provided for the traveller are the means by which they are achieved. From the designing of the hull to the navigation of the leviathan overseas, every process is full of interest, every step the result of carefully worked-out plans and infinitely minute precautions. The problem that confronts the naval architect called upon to design such a ship is a grave one. Not only is he required to plan a sumptuous hotel, but he must make a complex structure that will resist forces that none can appreciate but those who have faced the fury of an Atlantic storm.

The landsman, relying on his steamer to get him to London in time to keep a vital appointment, seldom stops to think that the graceful shape of the hull is one of the elements that makes a schedule possible. Before the keel of the thousand-foot floating palace is laid, toy steamers have been towed at certain speeds in a long tank to determine how much 'deadwood' must be cut away in order to allow the water to flow freely to propellers and rudder, lest half a knot of speed be lost.

Dimensions that will fit waterways and docks must be correlated with speed requirements contingent upon the limitations of space, for the power plant must not occupy room that could be utilized for the desired number of passengers, their baggage, and the necessary supplies for the voyage. The rolling and pitching of a great ship subject its frame to strains far greater than these ever put upon structures on land, and it must recover its normal shape after every strain. So, in the selection of materials, only such as will stretch one-fifth of their length before breaking are used. Poised on a wave as long as itself and half as high, the thousand-foot ship will have to withstand a bending strain of nearly 15 tons to the square inch. The Mauretania at these bending moments undergoes a strain calculated at 10.7 tons to the square inch, the bow and stern being at times almost clear of the water, when amidships, the vessel is sustained by its own buoyancy. Not less delicate than the calculation of strains is the fixing of engines, boilers, coal bunkers, outfit, cargo, and stores in the centres of gravity, and the adjustment of all so that the ship will trim on an even keel either when fully loaded or when nine-tenths empty. Every bit of space has its purpose. Even the double bottom is filled with water ballast, drinking water, and water for the boilers. Every inside nook must be used to provide for the comfort and safety of the passengers and crew, both with an eye to the economical use of space for cabins, staterooms, and promenades, and for the economical operation of the ship. A trifling improvement here, another there, makes every great vessel better than its predecessors in this respect. A sailor going to the masthead, for example, no longer has to risk his life by clambering up the quivering ratlines but ascends in safety by a spiral staircase inside the hollow steel mast.

On April 25, 1907, the Kaiser Wilhelm der Grosee was caught in a dense fog at about 50 deg. W. One hundred miles farther west was the Cunarder, Carmania. To a telegraphic enquiry as wind and weather; Carmania replied: – 'Light northerly winds, clear weather.' also stating her position about 12 miles farther south than the Kaiser, which now changed her course, and after steaming for six hours through the fog, reached clear weather as the Carmania had stated. In another heavy fog the Kaiser passed close by a steamer going in the same direction, only her sirens being heard. As she might have become dangerous to the Cunarder Caronia, which was on the same track, the captain of the German liner sent a wireless to the Caronia, 'Just passed a steamer close by, dense fog.' Two hours later the Caronia replied: 'Wind N.AV., weather clearing. Steamer close by.' This proved that the third steamer was on the course of the Caronia and might have collided with her.

Some maritime experts say that a good test of safety, furnishing proof of the elimination of danger in modern passenger ship construction, came in the autumn of 1911 when the White Star liner Olympic, crowded with home-coming Americans, was rammed by the British cruiser Hawke while in the Solent, off the Isle of Wight. The armoured prow of the warship struck the biggest ship ever built almost squarely at right angles. It tore a gaping hole in the liner's side, 'larger than a four-story house,' as one eyewitness put it, a hole that extended 20 feet below the water line. Although 10 years ago the wound would have sent any ship afloat to the bottom in as many minutes, it did not even prevent the Olympic from proceeding to the nearest port under her own power. So well did the system of water tight bulkheads and safety doors operate that the thousands of tons of water that poured in were kept in check, and only a slight settling by the stern gave evidence that the great ship was seriously hurt. Had the collision occurred in mid-ocean, instead of close to the shore, it is claimed that the Olympic would still have been able to make port in safety.

If that is so, this experience would seem to prove the theories of naval architects and constructors and to pave the way for even greater vessels. The simile of the skyscraper is appropriate to the thousand-foot ship, not only because of its size and character, but because of its method of construction. Like the building on shore, the ship of today is built on a skeleton steel frame that not only leaves room for machinery and cabins, but practically eliminates risks at sea. Since this method of construction gives the ship a double bottom, the inner shell of which is strong enough to float the craft if the outer is torn away, we hear no more of such ships being sunk by running on hidden rocks, derelicts, and icebergs.

Thirty or even 20 years ago the risk of collision with an iceberg was one the gravest perils of the sea, especially in the summer months when the ships were running at high speed on the short but foggy northern lane. Early in August 1911, the Anchor line Columbia came into the port of New York under her own power and only a few hours behind her schedule, with her whole bow stove in from a collision with an iceberg off the Grand Banks – an accident that would have sent any ship to the bottom a quarter of a century ago. The water-tight bulkheads that divide the greatest ship of today and will divide the greater ones of tomorrow into 20 or more compartments are strong enough to withstand any pressure from the outside, while if two or even three of them fill with water, the ship will still have reserve buoyancy enough to float and be navigated, as was proved in the case of the Olympic.

Longitudinal bulkheads will divide the thousand-foot ship lengthways, so that if the engines running one screw are disabled by water pouring in, there will still be power enough to proceed by means of a single screw, so long as the rudder is un damaged. And with the rudder gone, a great modern ship has been successfully steered across the Atlantic by means of the propeller alone. This was in October 1907, when the Kaiser Wilhelm der Grosse cracked her rudder soon after leaving New York. Halifax was only 700 miles away, and she might have put in there, but the captain decided to trust to the screws and took her across the Atlantic with the rudder entirely out of commission. Every corner of the thousand-foot ship will be connected by a system of electric nerves with the nerve centre under the captain's fingers, not only for the transmission of orders, but for the purpose of keeping him posted as to whether everything is working properly. On the modern liner water-tight doors that pierce the bulkheads are electrically connected with a diagram of the ship on the navigating bridge. By simply turning a lever at the bridge, the doors may be hydraulically closed and the ship hermetically sealed in 15 seconds. If any door fails to close, an electric bulb flashes and continues to burn until the door is closed. Thermostats in every part of the ship note the least rise in temperature above the danger mark and instantly notify the officer on watch by ringing a bell and flashing a red light. On a diagram he sees the exact location of the threatened fire and, as the bridge is the ship's telephone centre, he can summon assistance from the remotest parts. The thousand-foot ship will be, in short, practically fireproof and unsinkable and far safer than the ordinary modern hotel that has no means of isolating the point of origin of a fire or flooding itself with sea water at a moment's notice.

What will the thousand-foot ship cost? The estimate of two million pounds is, in the opinion of naval experts, none too high, even with all the facilities now available for its construction. The Olympic cost £1,500,000, and the thousand-footer will be nearly a third larger in bulk and consequently in cost. The Olympic is 105 ft. from the bottom of her keel to the top of her pilot house; 888 feet long. 92 feet wide, and displaces 60,000 tons of water, as against the Mauritania's 45.000. The thousand-foot ship will be more than 100 ft. wide and probably 140 ft. high and will have a tonnage displacement around 80.000. One of the difficulties that formerly blocked the way of the thousand-footer was the impossibility of moving such an immense mass off the launching ways by the old-fashioned methods that, even with smaller ships, frequently cost a number of human lives in the launching. But the whole vast weight of the Olympic was launched by the pressure of a button. A valve thus opened which released the hydraulic triggers which had been built even before the keel was laid. Some idea of the immensity of the thousand-foot ship may be gained by the size of some of the Olympic's parts. Her rudder alone weighs 100 tons. Each crank shaft weights 1.8 tons, each engine bed plate 195 tons, each engine column 21 tons, and the heaviest cylinder – 50 tons. The casting for her turbine cylinder weighed 167 tons. One of her solid bronze propellers weighs 22 tons and a single anchor 15 tons. Yet her reciprocating and turbine engines with, their 48,000 to 50,000 horsepower are designed to propel this ship at a speed of 21 nautical miles an hour, as against the Mauretania's 25 knots with 70,000 horse-power back of them – as much power as is required to turn the wheels of all the manufacturing plants and street railroads of a city the size of Rochester, New York, a lively American city of 218,000 population.'

Appendix III

WHY THE TITANIC WENT DOWN

The *Brisbane Telegraph* for 4 June 1912 published an article by Professor J H Biles giving his opinion concerning 'Unsinkable Ships':

> Professor Biles is vice-president of the Institution of Naval Architects and professor of naval architecture at Glasgow University; and his theories upon the causes of the sinking of the Titanic and his views as to the possibility of constructing an unsinkable ship may lie regarded as authoritative.
>
> The dreadful disaster to the Titanic naturally causes the public to ask the question, 'Can a ship be made which is unsinkable?' In order, to answer such a question, it is necessary to consider what keeps a ship afloat. A ship like the Titanic, weighing between 40,000 or 50,000 tons must lie supported by upward forces which in the aggregate are equal to the weight of the ship. A motor car weighing two tons resting on a road must be supported by an upward force from the road of two tons. If the surface of the road is not sufficiently strong to offer support of two tons, the car will sink into the road until somewhere under the surface it finds a sufficient upward force of two tons. A boy's solid wood boat sinks into the water of a pond until it finds an upward force equal to the weight of the boat. If the wood of the boat is, volume for volume, lighter than water, it will find its support without being wholly submerged.
>
> Nothing that can happen to this boat as it is can cause it to sink. It can only be caused to sink by weight, being added to it in the form of material whose weight is, volume for volume, heavier than water. In the case of a steel ship, the material of which it is constructed is, volume for volume, heavier than water. It is not solid like the boy's boat, but has large spaces partially filled with cargo or some other thing. It gets its support from the water, because it displaces a volume of water whose weight is equal to the weight of the ship. If the ship were not there a

143

volume of water equal to the volume of the ship would be there, and this volume would be supported by the pressure of the surrounding water. These pressures support a weight of water, equal in volume to that of the part of the ship that is under the water; and the same pressures exist when a ship is there. These pressures must support the weight of the ship. Whether the ship is there or not the pressures are the same, and they support the weight of the ship or the weight of the water displaced, according as either happens to be there. These two things, therefore, must be equal.

If the ship is damaged so that 'water' is allowed to enter her she must go further down into the water in order to displace more water and get support, not only for the weight she originally had, but for the weight of the water which has entered into her. If we could limit the extent to which the boat can be flooded by partitions placed round the hole, the amount of extra water carried could be made small and would only draw upon a small part of the out-water bulk of the boat for its support.

This method of limiting the extent of the flooding in a ship is called sub-division, and is given effect to by means of partitions made of steel plates suitably stiffened to resist water pressure. They are usually in one of three planes, either the horizontal parallel to the water surface; the vertical longitudinal plane, parallel to the keel of the ship; and transverse vertical plane, perpendicular to the keel of the ship.

The first, the horizontal, is represented by the decks and the inner bottom. The second, the vertical longitudinal, which is about 5 feet from the outer bottom, is represented by the sizes of coal bunkers and store-rooms. The third is represented by transverse bulkheads, which are divisions between boilers, machinery, cargo and passenger spaces. These partitions are made strong enough to prevent water passing through; and they serve the other purposes named. If the amount of sub-division necessary for the ordinary purposes of the ship is not enough to prevent the ship from sinking, when she has a definite amount of damage done to her outer skin, it is evident that more partitions must be put in until there is sufficient number to prevent her from sinking. In ships which are likely to be in collision with each other, a definite amount of damage is likely to be caused. The stem of a ship going into the side of another will make a hole of limited size; and if the vessel is divided into compartments small enough to be little larger than the extent of the damage, the localisation of the entry of water will be complete if the walls of the compartments are made strong enough to resist water pressure.

When, however, we have to deal with the question of damage other than by collision, the cause of it must be considered before arriving at any conclusion as to the possibility of making a ship unsinkable. If a ship is to receive damage throughout a considerable part of her length, so that the water would enter throughout this damaged part, a number of compartments might be flooded at the same time. The amount of flooding which a ship can stand without sinking must depend upon the amount of volume of the out-water portion, because, for every cubic foot of water that gets in the ship, she must sink bodily, so that the submerged part is a cubic foot more than before the water entered.

There is a further consideration – that the place where the water enters affects the level of the ship, and if it all enters at one end, that end must necessarily – down because the extra volume of displacement must be somewhere near the volume of water that enters. The ship may, therefore, be rendered quite unmanageable and may sink by getting a much smaller portion into the end than would be necessary to sink her if admitted nearer the middle. Therefore, if a definite amount of damage is done, there must be greater sub-division if that damage is in the ends of a ship than if it is in the middle of her length. It is quite possible to determine, in every case, to what line a ship would sink if a given amount of her flooded.

If the question of how much of the ship is likely to be flooded cannot be easily determined, if provision is being made against collision with another ship, the extent of the damage and the extent of the length of the ship which will be flooded can be predicted with a fair amount of certainty. But if she is to run onto a rock or is to butt into an iceberg or a cliff, it would be difficult to determine to what extent the damage would go. A still more severe test is that of making a glancing blow on a rock or on an iceberg which would rip up a long length of side, when there would be a very much larger provision of sub-division necessary.

If a ship is to be built to remain afloat after the whole of one side is ripped up, it must be more costly to build than existing vessels; she would be very much more difficult to be made use of and to work. As far as utility is concerned, sub-division reaches its limit when the main division of the machinery, cargo, and passenger spaces are subdivided from each other by these partitions. Any further additions which are made must be to add to the safety of the ship, and the whole question is one of compromise between utility and safety. In warships, which have a very much larger amount of sub-division than merchant ships, the limit of utility is much further along the line of numbers of compartments in the former than the latter, because there are so many things that have to be separated from each other. Even with the larger extent of sub-division in worships, they have been sunk in collision and by gunfire when it has been of sufficient extent to flood enough compartments.

The sub-division of the Titanic has been enough to enable her to remain afloat for four hours after collision with an iceberg. It is impossible, without further knowledge of the circumstances of the collision, to say if a greater amount of sub-division would have enabled her to remain afloat longer. She had fifteen main transverse bulkheads, which is a very large number for a passenger steamer. She might, however, have had more, for in two vessels of the Inman line built more than two years ago (for whose designs I was responsible) there were as many; though the vessels were not much more than half the length of the Titanic.

The increase in length does not necessitate increase in numbers of compartments to produce the same safety. On the contrary, the larger vessel is rather safer because she is not liable to get an amount of damage in proportion to her length. There is no doubt, however, that increased sub-division does increase the chance of escape. The risk that is run of collision with ice appears to be very small, judging by the results. But the dangers which follow such a collision are so much greater than those which follow the collision with another steamer (bad as they are) that the subject must be most fully investigated.

John Harvard Biles was born in Portsmouth in 1854. He served his apprenticeship at Portsmouth dockyard, and graduated from the Royal Naval College at Greenwich in 1875. He joined the Admiralty, and in 1880 he was appointed chief designer at J and G Thomson's Clydebank shipyard. He was professor of Naval Architecture at the University of Glasgow from 1891 to 1922. He continued to work as a consultant during his tenure of the University chair, often involving his students in these commissions. His work on numerous government committees, and valuable service rendered to the Admiralty in the development of the Dreadnought warships and other projects led to the award of a knighthood in 1913, and his being awarded an LLD, and the appointment of KCIE (Knight Commander of the Indian Empire) in 1922. He died at Virginia Water in Surrey on 27 October 1933.

HOW THE MAIL STEAMER WENT DOWN IN MID-ATLANTIC, BY A SURVIVOR
By W T Stead

We took in 158 mail bags and 342 passengers at Queenstown, and there was a good deal of confusion as the steamer headed away to the west, for we had shipped 560 passengers in all at Liverpool, and it was a pretty tight fit in the steerage. I stayed on deck till after eleven at night.

'She's going it,' I said, by way of the opening conversation. 'Yes, by the hokey, she's doing sixteens now, and if the wind only comes round she'll score eighteens like a winking.'

'It's rather thick to drive her, isn't it?'

'Thick be blowed. We ain't got to mind that much. We shall slow her down a bit if we blunder into a regular fog, but she can't spare a yard. Reckon we shall average seventeens right across.

'Our talk went on till curtain of midnight was fairly folded round us, and then I went aft to lend a hand with the log. Sure enough we were going sixteens and our progress was rather like that of a mackerel than a ship.

The enormous pulse of the engines sent great tremors from stem to stern, and at every wheeling lash of the propeller the boat thrust her way through the black mountains that came down on her, tossing their savage white crests. In the morning the gale blew harder, and the decks were almost deserted save by the few seasoned hands who came up to smoke in the alleys. It was not till the fourth day we had a fine spell of sunshine, and from the fore hatch to the spare wheel the deck was crammed with jostling lines of pale but cheerful people.

147

I did not much like the appearance of our Liverpool lot. I had an intermediate ticket, but I wandered among the steerage company without much interruption until I happened to stumble against one of the English roughs.

I begged pardon, but the surly fellow said: 'What be'est moochin' round here for? Say, Curly, see this blank swine majorin' round's zif the place b'longed to 'im. I'll give you my toe, my joker, 'fore you can say knife if you come that agin!'

I said: 'I've asked your pardon, my man, and I assure you it was an accident. As for your toe, I advise you not to try it on. I have a full allowance of toes and boots.'

He was a fellow with that type of snake head which denotes the fighting man; his jowl was vast, the point of his jaw was covered by the strained skin which showed how he was clenching his teeth; and his evil little eyes looked venomous under his rugged, bestial brows.

He said: 'Do you know who I am? I'm Jim Cormick and I'm going out to spar with the Boston Boy.'

I was not much alarmed, though I saw that his fist would mark me if he got home. His friends came round, and I am bound to say that they were as unpleasant a lot as you can meet. There was no sign of discipline among the 560 steerage passengers, though it is fair to say that the foreigners behaved admirably. When a vessel hove up there was a nasty rush to the side where she could be seen, and the women had to get out of the way as best they could. The officers' uniforms cowed the most offensive of the rowdies, but I don't think the terror was very deep-seated. The after-cabin passengers were a nice lot, and I particularly admired some of the ladies who came out in their sea rig, and made the deck gay. One Englishman of distinction attracted me strangely. He had his wife and family with him, and a more beautiful group I never saw. The eldest girl was a dark beauty about eighteen years of age, and it was a pretty sight to see the father beau-ing her about. The time went by pleasantly enough with us all, but I did wish that some sort of discipline could have been established among the more blackguardly males, for their games were senseless and offensive.

On the fifth night out the moon shown beautifully, and we were surrounded by a fireworks of silver. I could not sleep for the very delight of living, and I walked up and down crooning over old rhymes under the glad mystery of the night. A sudden freak prompted me to hoist myself up from the alley, and I had a look at four of the boats. The hole-pins were laid ready, water casks made fast forward, oars lashed handily, plugs out. I counted the thwarts, and it struck me that the other four boats must be pretty big, for the four amidships were certainly small enough. At the finish I calculated that, by leading all the eight boats down to the water's edge and packing the children along the bottom boards, we might accommodate 390 people. We were carrying 916 altogether.

The next morning at three o'clock I felt restless; so I came up, and found that we were lunging over a long, true sea, that moved in grey hillocks under a thick haze. It was not really a fog, but it was puzzling.

The look-out man sang shrilly, 'Vessel away on the starboard bow, sir.'

'All right.' We steamed on, and I watched the looming ship.

'Shows his green, sir!'

'All right.'

A minute after the boatswain ran swiftly aft, and said softly to the officer on the bridge: 'He's going about, sir. D–d if I know what he wants to do.'

We lost sight of the vessel's green just as we cleared the big bank of haze, and then I saw that a big barque was standing right across our bows. I glanced at the mate, and saw him compress his lips; then I saw that we were edging away to port, and I knew that our man was going to shoot across the barque's bows. Distances are so deceptive that I still had no thought of nervousness till the barque suddenly shook out her square mainsail and came surging away till we saw her red light. What could one make of this? The officer yelled of a sudden, with an oath, 'Starboard, for Christ's sake, starboard!' and then, as if by magic, the cloud of canvas seemed to overtop us. I saw the officer hanging to the rail, and as I jumped on the hatches I noticed, with forlorn curiosity, that his knuckles were white. I heard a long scrunch, and then the barque bounded back a few yards, while the steamer trailed on; she came slowly into us again, and I heard her bows crashing, for she had dashed clean against the bulks of the stokehole. One shrill scream came shuddering up from the cabin – only one – then a murmur, then a hoarse burst of yelling; then a man came up and cried, 'Oh, my God!' and then, in a wild, remorseless, ferocious crowd, the steerage men trampled up, struggling, tearing each other's clothes, cursing, praying. Some of the women battered and screamed as they tried to force the bolts of their door; then the whole crowd broke clear, and soon they were clinging to the men, praying, jabbering with notes of horrible pathos all kinds of incoherences. I ran aft, and saw the barque waver, lurch, and then sink.

I remember now observing how her masts quivered, and I heard a report like that of heavy cannon as her hatches were thrust up by the air. A green and white mountain gleamed in the grey of the dawn, and then the ship was no more seen. The ladies from the cabin were mostly in their nightdresses, and the men also had taken no time to dress. I saw white, drawn faces, and I noticed particularly my English gentleman and his daughter. She was hanging to his arm, and I thought she was shaking convulsively, but she kept her lips tight, and only the deadly stare of her eyes flashing from the pallor of her writhing face told of her trouble. The captain rushed forward, buckling his belt as he came. He was in his shirt sleeves, and I saw the butt of a Derringer peeping from his Yankee pocket behind him. From below there came a queer sucking sound, with an occasional long gurgle, and I saw that the vessel seemed to 'hang' as the seas met her. The second officer, who was a smart man, had passed a spare sail over the side, and I knew he wanted to reeve it under her, but he might just as well have tried to stop the middle arch of London Bridge. The engines were still kept going, but the deck slanted, slanted steadily, and the list to starboard reached an angle that made it difficult to stand at all, especially as the uneasy, staggering lunges of the steamer were taking her anyhow. An awkward rush of men swayed forward; the boxer and his gang made a desperate attempt to get one of the boats clear; cursing and praying, they hacked at the tackles with knives; some of them swarmed up, and stood on the thwarts tearing savagely at the chains; but the boats were made fast to stand heavy weather, and only skilled sailors could launch them. A loud crack, followed by a wallowing noise like thunder, rendered all other sounds insignificant, and a captain who was going out to New York said; 'The bulkhead's gone. We must take our chance now.' The ship stopped nearly dead, and began to tremble curiously, but that was only the river of water pouring aft, and we soon saw the firemen driven up like rats from a burrow. 'Stand by the boats!'

The order was given, and the boatswain's call rose in a long, tremulous screech. The sailors tried to get to their quarters, and I observed that their occasional drills had done them good. But then the drills had been carried on while the passengers stood aloof, so that the sailors were used to having their own way. At this juncture there was a maddened host of cowardly men and hysterical women to be dealt with. I forced my way forward toward one of the starboard boats, and as I thrust my way through the crush, an Irish woman clung to me with one arm, while she held up a shivering baby with the other. The woman was nearly naked, but she never heeded the cold.

'Mother of God,' she cried, 'take my little one, and make sure of him.'

I shook her off and pushed on. A terrified navvy sought to keep me back, and he scratched at my face like a cat; but I reached the davits. The men had the boat swung round, and the carpenter was about to let her run, when a mixed mob of English and foreigners took possession, and in an instant the little craft was packed with a weltering heap of men who had quite lost their senses. I saw the captain leave the bridge with a flying spring, and I saw also the gleam of the pistol barrels; then I heard on the starboard side the rapid 'Smash, smash' of a revolver shot, and the captain shouted, 'You hear what they're getting on the other side! Out of it, or I take you one after the other.' The sailors were fighting hard, but the men in the boat fought also with the oars and boathooks; one seaman had his head split; another received a wound from a boathook which took his cheek away in one nasty flap.

Still the ruffians did not know how to lower away, and one of them began to lash at the forward fall with an axe.

'Come down, you sir.'

'You be d—d.'

Crack! The man flung up his arms, dropped his axe, and fell headlong into the sea.

'Now down with you,' said the captain, livid and half-blind with fury.

But no. A furious fool succeeded in letting the boat go by the head and the whole crowd of poltroons were dumped into the swashing sea, where they gasped and struggled till the last two men throttled each other and rolled under. One of the starboard boats was successfully launched, and the chief officer stood, revolver in hand.

'Women first here. Thompson, you will steer her. Take four men and no more.'

The young English lady was lowered down, although she clung hard to her father and begged him to let her stay.

'No, darling. Goodbye. Be happy!' he said, and then stood composedly amid the hurly-burly.

A pretty actress and two Irish women were next sent down; then four children were put in, and then the sailors sprang over the side and prepared to help others.

An Irishman shouted, 'Now, boys!' His voice seemed to send an impulse through the crowd, and the roughs tore themselves away from the women, and flung themselves recklessly – some into the boat, some into the water. The officer fired two barrels and missed each time; a sailor shoved off, and we saw an over-laden boat lumber heavily away astern.

All this scene of horror took place in less than two minutes, and the ship settled more and more every second. The prize fighter and his gang were not successful in their attempt to steal the boat forward. The purser and the steward armed themselves with firemen's rods and beat the fellows down; then the baker – a quick young lad, who

151

had learned his business as a seaman in addition to his trade – let the boat slip, and four gallant men withstood the ferocious rowdies until eighteen women had been pitched over the side and carelessly lowered. A seaman took the tiller, four stokers, the purser, and the baker jumped in at the last moment, and this second boat went adrift. Meanwhile the captain had reloaded – alas! What a pity he only had two barrels – and a third and fourth boat went off with half their proper complement. Another boatload might have escaped, but six men sprang from the port side, and actually stove the cutter in. At last, only one light boat remained, and still there were over 700 of us jammed in the narrow space left by the awful list. The captain had dropped his hands; he could do no more. The third mate took a handspike and went smashing among the men who were wrestling around our last hope.

One sailor said, 'We've stood it long enough, Tom. Let's have our turn.' And he, with three sturdy Swedes, managed to get at the davits. They were just in time, for the steamer began to sway as they floated, and they flung themselves into the water. Then I was left with a great multitude, whose agonized clamour stunned me. I felt a mighty, convulsive movement; then the sea seemed to flash down on me in one mass, as if the wall of water fell from a high crag. Then I heard a humming noise in my ears, and with a gasp I was up amid a blackened, wriggling sheet of drowning creatures. A boat came past me, and I struck out lustily. I raised myself to the gunwale.

'Shall I hit his fingers,' said a man.

'No, let him come,' and then I was laid, sick and dizzy, on the bottom boards of a crowded boat. You know that we were picked up after a nasty time, and I am at home minus my kit.

THE BROMPTON CEMETERY EGYPTIAN TOMB

Appreciation of ancient Egyptian culture and aesthetics enjoyed a great revival in the nineteenth century and held a fascination with Victorians and Edwardians, and it was fashionable to engrave their signs and symbols on cemetery monuments. Some examples are the entrance to Abney Park Cemetery in Stoke Newington, which was built in Egyptian style; Highgate Cemetery boasts an imposing Egyptian-style gate leading into the Egyptian Avenue; and the gates of the catacombs in Brompton Cemetery are adorned with scarab beetles with Egyptian serpents curling around staffs which are a symbol of eternal life, of which some believe the Pharaohs had discovered the secret.

The Kilmorey Mausoleum was a massive pink and grey granite structure with a bronze door built at Brompton Cemetery in the Egyptian manner, and dedicated to Osiris, the god of resurrection. It was commissioned by an eccentric named Francis Jack Needham, 2nd Earl of Kilmorey, for the burial of his mistress, Priscilla Ann Hoste, who died of heart disease on 21 October 1854, and included an empty casket with a blank nameplate intended for him. It stood at circle number 1 near the main entrance at the northern end of the cemetery. Kilmorey was an occultist, and believed it would serve as a portal to the underworld. It was moved to Woburn Park in about 1862.

Another Egyptian connection to the cemetery is the grave of a surgeon named Thomas Joseph 'Mummy' Pettigrew, an archaeological expert on Egyptian mummies, who became well-known in London social circles for his private meetings at his surgery in Saville Row, or at his house in Brompton, in which he used to unroll mummies and perform autopsies on the exposed body parts. He was a founding member of the British Archaeological Society in 1843, and during its first meeting he unrolled a mummy as part of the programme of events. He died on 23 November 1865, aged 74.

Adorned in even more symbolism is the mausoleum of the mysterious, somewhat adventurous, Hannah Courtoy, one of the most imposing crypts in London, and the largest construction in the cemetery, after the Kilmorey tomb had been removed. It stands away from the majority of graves around it, and towers twenty feet over them. Its polished walls of dark granite are also decorated in Egyptian symbolism of eternal life, and hieroglyphics. It features a pyramid-style top, and the solid bronze doors are covered in Egyptian markings. There are strange motifs along the bottom of the door, and a large circular hole in the top, with eight smaller holes surrounding it. It has been suggested that a type of clock or dial was once fitted there.

Some details of Hannah's life can be found, but much of it is speculation. She was born as Hannah Peters in Westminster in about 1784. Her father was named Peter, and Hannah was forced to leave home in 1799 to escape his abusive and drunken behaviour.

It seems she had many lovers. Two members of the House of Hanover are said to have made her their royal mistress, and she may have even married a man called Robert Francis Grosso, who introduced her to an extremely rich much older Frenchman named John Courtoy, whose real name was Nicholas Jacquinet. He is said to have been a wig-maker and hairdresser, but had made a fortune as a merchant and money-lender during the French Revolution, and that may have been why he had to change his name and move to London. He was one of the one hundred richest people in England at the beginning of the nineteenth century, but was reputed to have been a miser with his money. Hannah became his housekeeper – and then his lover.

Hannah had three daughters. Mary Ann was baptised at St James's Church in Piccadilly on 22 March 1802; Elizabeth was born in 1804; and Susannah was baptised at St Martin's-in-the-Field in Westminster on 13 January 1807. Official documentation records that on 3 August 1821 the Courtoy family tried to gain custody of the girls, because on 21 December that year Hannah was arrested and held at Fleet Prison to answer their statements.

John Courtoy was interested in Egyptology and the diaries of a Courtoy servant who befriended Hannah state that Joseph Bonomi the Younger, a well-known sculptor and Egyptologist of the time, visited the Courtoy household because he had expressed a desire to help finance Bonomi's expeditions to Egypt and the pyramids. It was Bonomi who designed the entrance to Abney Park Cemetery soon after it opened in 1840, with hieroglyphics signifying the cemetery as being 'The Abode of the Mortal Part of Man' – another suggestion of eternal life, and he is believed to have been among the first to decipher some of the hieroglyphs found in the Valley of the Kings.

It is thought that John Courtoy left no will to his estate when he died on 8 December 1818, although one did come to light, possibly forged, and although it was contested by members of the Courtoy family because he was never legally married to Hannah, she and her daughters inherited most of the fortune. They followed lavish social lifestyles thereafter, and at the time of the first census held in 1841, Hannah and her two unmarried daughters, Mary Ann and Elizabeth, were living at 14 Wilton Crescent in the exclusive upmarket London district of Belgrave Square, where Hannah remained for the rest of her life.

A cholera epidemic attacked London from about 1848 to 1852, and Hannah died from the disease on 26 January 1849. According to the burial register she was aged 65. She was originally placed in the East Bell Tower Catacombs on 13 February 1849, and, such was the family's influence – or a financial offer the cemetery authorities could not refuse – that on 30 January 1849 they allowed Mary and Elizabeth to purchase the whole of the ground in the area which made up what was then circle number 3. Some of the circles remain to this day, and actually form part of the pathway. Hannah was finally laid to rest in the tomb on 13 March 1852.

In the following month, Joseph and Jessie Bonomi lost four children to the same disease, and they were buried close to Hannah. The tragedy took its toll on Jessie. She died in 1859, and was buried with them.

Because of Bonomi's association with John Courtoy, it has been suggested that he helped to design the mausoleum, although there is no existing documentation to say that he did. However, it may be that he *had* worked in that area and chose it as a gravesite for his children soon after Hannah had been interred, with the desire to have them buried close to such an impressive monument displaying symbolism close to his heart. There are some Egyptian symbols on his headstone; including a depiction of Hannah's tomb, but it seems that despite his distinguished career, he was happy to be buried in the same relatively ordinary grave as his wife and children, satisfied that it was in view of such a fantastic mausoleum.

If Bonomi did help to design the tomb, it is said that he was influenced by a former sea captain named Samuel Alfred Warner, who once tried to dupe the British military into financing two far-too-advanced –

and far-fetched – inventions. The navy were interested enough to allow Warner to blow up a ship during a test of one of his ideas, a kind of torpedo, but the armaments turned out to be frauds.

The suggestion is that Bonomi had discovered the secret of time travel from the hieroglyphs he had read on one of his expeditions. Supposedly, the two men convinced Hannah that it was possible to travel in time, and suggested they start a secret project to build a mausoleum that would actually be a time machine, and they would place it in a cemetery since such places rarely changed and they could work unobserved for most of the time. A few months after Hannah had been placed in the crypt, Warner died in Pimlico, apparently under suspicious circumstances, aged 59, and was buried in a common grave in a different part of the cemetery on 10 December 1853. Some say he died in connection with something he discovered while working on the construction, while others accuse Bonomi of murdering him to stop him from telling anyone about their project. It has also been suggested that the Courtoys, Bonomi and Warner are still alive to this day as eternal life time-travellers.

Bonomi's connection with Abney Park has led to speculation that the reasons why the Courtoy tomb took so long to finish is because he and Warner were constructing and connecting either the suggested time portal or a teleportation machine connected with similar such devices in other London cemeteries. The purpose being to create a transportation grid from one crypt to another to reduce the time taken to travel around the Metropolis, where the streets were becoming more and more congested each year.

Mary and Elizabeth remained unmarried and living at the same house in Wilton Crescent. Mary died on 5 January 1868, aged 67, and was placed in the tomb on 14 January, and Elizabeth died on 31 August 1876, aged 72. Susannah married a barrister named Septimus Holmes Godson (1799–1877), at St George's Church in Hanover Square, on 21 June 1830, and made up for her sisters' lack of offspring by having at least thirteen children. They lived at 14 Rutland Gate near Hyde Park, and Susannah died on 11 January 1895, aged 88. She was buried with her husband in the East Terrace, an area that is no longer part of the cemetery. Joseph Bonomi became curator of the Sir John Soanes's Museum in Holborn. He had twelve children in all. He died on 3 March 1878, aged 81, and was buried with his family.

Speculation that the Courtoy mausoleum is a portal to other time dimensions has caused considerable curiosity for many years. Although it is thought that the door to the tomb has not been opened since 1876, according to the Brompton burial register, the last time it was opened was on 16 February 1981, when 89-year-old Edwin Godson, a barrister of Chelsea, who was a descendant of Susannah and had researched into his family's history, became the fourth person to be placed inside, because the Godson grave situated elsewhere in the cemetery was full. It seems that since then the key has gone astray, and it would take the work of a skilled heritage locksmith to gain entry into what is now a grade II listed monument.

BIBLIOGRAPHY AND RESEARCH SOURCES

A & E Television Networks, *Titanic: The Complete Story* (TV Documentary), 1994

Amazon Ship, *The Lost Steamer: A History of the Amazon*, 1852

Ancestry.co.uk

Atlantic Daily Bulletin, The Journal of the British Titanic Society

Australasia newspaper, 14 August 1909

Ballard, Robert Duane, *The Discovery of the Titanic*, 1987

Bancroft, James W, *Titanic: Iceberg Ahead – The Story of the Disaster by Some of Those Who Were There*, 2021

Bartlett, W B, *Titanic: 9 Hours to Hell, the Survivors' Story*, 2011

Behe, George, *Titanic: Psychic Forewarnings of a Tragedy*, 1988

Beesley, Lawrence, *The Loss of the SS Titanic: Its Story and Its Lessons*, 1912

Belfast Titanic Society

Bell, Chief Engineer Joseph, Letter to his son written on 11 April 1912

Bingham, Randy Bryan; and Jasper, Gregg, Broadway Dame, *The Life and Times of Mrs Henry B Harris*, 2019

Board of Trade, *The Investigation into the Loss of the SS Titanic*, 1912

Borderland: A Quarterly Review and Index of Psychic Phenomena, 1893–1897

Brisbane Telegraph, 4 June 1912

Brisbane Truth, 11 January 1953

British Government, *Loss of the Steamship Titanic: Report of a Formal Investigation into the Circumstances Attending the Foundering on April 15, 1912 of the British Steamship Titanic, of Liverpool, After Striking Ice in or near Latitude 41 – 46 N; Longitude 50 – 14 W, North Atlantic Ocean, as Conducted by the British Government*, 1912

Brown, Rustie, *Titanic: The Psychic and the Sea*, 1981

Bryceson, Dave, *The Titanic Disaster as Reported in the British National Press, April–July 1912*, 1997

Butt, Archibald W, *Taft and Roosevelt: The Intimate Letters of Archie Butt, Military Aide* (2 volumes), 1930

Census Returns, 1841–1921

Chirnside, Mark, *The 'Olympic' Class Ships*, 2004

Cooper, Gary J, *Titanic Captain: The Life of Edward John Smith*, 2011

Cooper, Gary J, *The Man Who Sank the Titanic: The Life and Times of Captain Edward Smith*

Daily Mirror, 10 January 1998, 19 April 1912 and 10 October 1936

Daugherty, Greg, *Seven Famous People Who Missed the Titanic. Smithsonian Magazine*, 2012

Encyclopedia Titanica

Findmypast

Gardiner, Robin, *Titanic: The Ship That Never Sank,* 1998

Gardner, Martin, *The Wreck of the Titanic Foretold*, 1998

Grace's Guide to British Industrial Industry

Gracie IV, Colonel Archibald, *the Truth About the Titanic*, 1913

Hall, Steve; Beveridge, Bruce; Braunschweiger Art, *Titanic or Olympic: Which Ship Sank? The Truth behind the Conspiracy*, 2012

Harland and Wolff Director's Minute Book held in the Public Records Office

Haworth, Rodger, *Miramar Ship Index*

Hoff, Gill, *The Sinking of RMS Tailyour: The Lost Story of the Victorian Titanic*

Holman, Hannah, *Titanic Voices: 63 Survivors Tell Their Extraordinary Stories*, 2011

Hyslop, Donald; Forsyth, Alastair; Jemima, Sheila, *Titanic Voices: Memories from the Fateful Voyage*, 1994

Illustrated London News, 4 May 1912

Iversen, Kristen, *Molly Brown: Unravelling the Myth, the True Life Story of the Titanic's Most Famous Survivor*, 1999

Jefferson, Herbert, *Viscount Pirrie of Belfast*, 1948

Jessop, Violet and Maxtone-Graham, John, *The Memoirs of Violet Jessop, Stewardess*, 1998

Journal of the Society for Psychical Research, volume 15, 1912

JWB Historical Library

Keefe, Terry, *Premonitions of the Titanic Disaster*, 2021

Kurin, Richard, *Hope Diamond: the Legendary History of a Cursed Gem*, 2006

Launceston Examiner, 19 October 1898

Lightoller, Charles Herbert, *Titanic and Other Ships*, 1935

London Evening Standard, 25 January 1854, *The Wreck of the Taylyeur*

Lord, Walter, *A Night to Remember*, 1955

Lord, Walter, *The Night Lives On*: *Thoughts, Theories and Revelations about the Titanic*, 1986

Lynch, Don, *Titanic – An Illustrated History*, 1992

Matsen, Bradford, *Titanic's Last Secrets*, 2006

Meheust, Bertrand, *Histoires Paranormales Du Titanic (Paranormal Stories from the Titanic)*, 2006

Meissner, Sophie Radford de, *There Are No Dead*, 1912

Meissner, Sophie Radford de, *Old Naval Days. Sketches from the life of Rear-Admiral William Radford, USN*, 1920

Merseyside Maritime Museum

Middlesex Gazette, 20 April 1912

Molony, Senan, *The Irish aboard Titanic*, 2012

Moss, Michael S and John R Hume, *Shipbuilders to the World: 125 Years of Harland and Wolf, Belfast, 1861–1986*, 1986

National Archives

National Maritime Museum

National Museums, Liverpool

Occult Review, 20 February 1913

Oldham, Wilton J, *The Ismay Line: The White Star Line and the Ismay Family Story*, 1961

Pellow, James; and Kendle, Dorothy, *a Lifetime on the Titanic: A Biography of Edith Haisman*, 1995

Perth Guardian, 21 March to 12 April 1947

Pleasants, Helene (editor), Biographical Dictionary of Parapsychology, 1964

Prior, Melton, *Campaigns of a War Correspondent*, 1912

Reynold's Newspaper, 21 April 1912

Robertson, Morgan Andrew, *Gathering No Moss*

Robinson, W Sydney, *Muckraker: The Scandalous Life and Times of W T Stead. Britain's First Investigative Journalist*

Rostron, Sir Arthur Henry, *Home from the Sea*, 1931

Sheil, Inger, *Titanic Valour: The Life of Fifth Officer Harold Lowe*, 2012

Society of Naval Architects and Marine Engineers: *Titanic: The Anatomy of a Disaster: A*

Report from the Marine Forensic Panel, 1997

Russell, Thomas H, *Sinking of the Titanic: the World's Greatest Sea Disaster*, 1912

Scott, J W Robertson, *The Life and Death of a Newspaper: An Account of the Temperaments, Perturbations, and achievements of John Morley, W T Stead, E T Cook, Harry Cust, J L Garvin and three other Editors of the Pall Mall Gazette*, 1952

Sheffield Daily Telegraph, 19 July and 23 August 1919; 28 August 1920; 9 April, 16 July, 3 December 1921; 8 April 1922; 17 May 1930

Southampton City Heritage Oral History

Southampton Times and Hampshire Express, 20 April 1912

The Sphere, 4 May 1912

Stead, Estelle W, *My Father: Spiritual and Personal Reminiscences*, 1913

Stead, Estelle W, *The Blue Island: Experiences of a New Arrival beyond the Veil*, 1922

Stenson, Patrick: *Titanic Voyage: The Odyssey of C H Lightoller*, 1998

Sunday Independent, 15 April 1962

Sweetingham, Clive, *Slade Brothers: The Real Story*. Encyclopaedia Titanica.

Sydney Truth, 26 August 1951

Thayer III, John Borland 'Jack', *The Sinking of the SS Titanic, April 14–15 1912*, 1940

Ticehurst, Brian, *The Titanic's Rescuers: Captain, Sir Arthur Rostron and the Crew of the* Carpathia, 1996

The Times, 21 April 1912

Titanic Commutator, The Journal of Titanic Historical Society

Titanic Historical Society

Titanic International Society

Town and Country Journal, 3 June 1914

Turner, General, Sir Alfred Edward, *Sixty Years of a Soldier's Life*, 1912

Turner, Steve, *The Band That Played On: The Extraordinary Story of the 8 Musicians Who Went Down With the Titanic*, 2011

United States Enquiry: *Investigation into the Loss of the SS Titanic*, 1912

University of Glasgow

Vancouver Daily Province, 2 May 1912

Villiers, Frederic, *His Five Decades of Adventure* (volume 2), 1920

Ward, Christopher, *And the Band Played On. The Titanic Violinist and the Glove-Maker, A True Story of Love, Loss and Betrayal*, 1911

Whiteley, Thomas: *Titanic Lecture*

Whiting, Lilian, *The Adventure Beautiful*, 1917

Wilson, Andrew, *Shadow of the Titanic: The Extraordinary Stories of Those Who Survived*, 2012

Winocour, Jack, *The Story of the Titanic, as told by its Survivors*, 1960

W T Stead Resource Site

INDEX